UNDERSTANDING ASSESSMENT IN COUNSELLING AND PSYCHOTHERAPY

Other books in this series

What is Counselling & Psychotherapy?
by Norman Claringbull   ISBN 978 1 84445 361 0

**Counselling and Psychotherapy in Organisational
Settings** edited by Judy Moore and Ruth Roberts   ISBN 978 1 84445 614 7

**Creating the Therapeutic Relationship in
Counselling and Psychotherapy** by Judith Green   ISBN 978 1 84445 463 1

Effective Counselling with Young People
by Hazel Reid and Jane Westergaard   ISBN 978 0 85725 295 1

Mental Health in Counselling and Psychotherapy
by Norman Claringbull   ISBN 978 0 85725 377 4

**Reflective Practice in Counselling and
Psychotherapy** by Sofie Bager-Charleson   ISBN 978 1 84445 360 3

Books in the Mental Health in Practice series

**Cognitive Behavioural Interventions for Mental
Health Practitioners** edited by Alec Grant   ISBN 978 1 84445 210 1

Mental Health Law in England and Wales
by Paul Barber, Robert Brown and Debbie Martin   ISBN 978 1 84445 195 1

To order, please contact our distributor: BEBC Distribution, Albion Close, Parkstone, Poole, BH12 3LL. Telephone 0845 230 9000, email: **learningmatters@bebc.co.uk**. You can also find more information on each of these titles and our other learning resources at **www.learningmatters.co.uk**

Want to write for the Counselling and Psychotherapy Practice series? Contact the Commissioning Editor, Luke Block (Luke@learningmatters.co.uk), with your ideas and proposals.

UNDERSTANDING ASSESSMENT IN COUNSELLING AND PSYCHOTHERAPY

SOFIE BAGER-CHARLESON AND
BILJANA VAN RIJN

Series editor: Norman Claringbull

First published in 2011 by Learning Matters Ltd

All rights reserved. No part of this publication may be reproduced, stored in a retrieval system, or transmitted in any form or by any means, electronic, mechanical, photocopying, recording, or otherwise, without prior permission in writing from Learning Matters.

© Sofie Bager-Charleson and Biljana van Rijn 2011

British Library Cataloguing in Publication Data
A CIP record for this book is available from the British Library.

ISBN: 978 0 85725 473 3

This book is also available in the following ebook formats:

Adobe ebook   ISBN: 978 0 85725 475 7
ePUB ebook   ISBN: 978 0 85725 474 0
Kindle   ISBN: 978 0 85725 476 4

The rights of Sofie Bager-Charles and Biljana van Rijn to be identified as the Authors of this Work have been asserted by them in accordance with the Copyright, Designs and Patents Act 1988.

Cover design by Code 5 Design Associates
Project management by Diana Chambers
Typeset by Kelly Winter
Printed and bound in Great Britain by Short Run Press Ltd, Exeter, Devon

Learning Matters Ltd
20 Cathedral Yard
Exeter EX1 1HB
Tel: 01392 215560
info@learningmatters.co.uk
www.learningmatters.co.uk

Contents

	Foreword	vi
	Acknowledgements	viii
	About the authors	ix
	Introduction	1
Chapter 1	The role of the assessor in private practice	8
Chapter 2	'Diagnosing' problems	44
Chapter 3	Treatment – illuminating shaded areas?	64
Chapter 4	Assessment in organisations: an overview	77
Chapter 5	Conducting an assessment	91
Chapter 6	Assessment skills	110
Appendix 1	Initial assessment form used by the Metanoia Counselling and Psychotherapy Service	125
	References	128
	Index	135

Foreword

Many counsellors and psychotherapists worry whether assessment is a subject with which they ever have any right, or any need, to concern themselves. Very often, therapists are unhappy about making judgements about their clients. To them, perhaps, assessment does not seem like a proper activity for counsellors and psychotherapists. On the other hand, some therapists decide that it is quite proper to assess clients, which leads to another concern, namely, how can therapists effectively go about assessment in ways that help their clients and which avoid harming them?

Many modern counsellors and psychotherapists regularly carry out client assessments. Some of these practitioners may have decided that such an investigatory process is a useful part of their routine therapeutic work. Others may have found themselves required to carry out assessments by their employing organisations and agencies. In any event, if you want to develop your client assessment skills, then you will find this book of enormous benefit. You will find a lot of very useful theory-based discussion about the various approaches to assessment and you will also find that it is full of practical information, activities, key concepts and case studies.

The authors are two experienced teachers and practitioners of counselling and psychotherapy. This is what makes their book such a valuable contribution to the *Counselling and Psychotherapy Practice* series. Any therapist, at any level, from initial trainee to advanced practitioner, can learn a lot from Sofie and Biljana. They boldly begin their book by telling us a lot about themselves. Such a courageous beginning not only helps us to understand much better where they are coming from, but it also helps us to better evaluate what they tell us. In other words, Sofie and Biljana invite their readers to begin their own individual voyages into client assessment by first assessing their teachers. After all, as they remind us throughout their text, assessment is a reflexive business.

Assessment is best if it is a flexible process; one that is continuously revisited throughout the therapeutic engagement. After all, if we want our clients to become 'unfixed', should not we be prepared keep our ideas about them 'unfixed' too? For many practitioners, assessment helps to give purpose to counselling and psychotherapy. This is because they believe that assessment gives them some benchmarks from which they can measure their professional effectiveness. However, as Sofie and Biljana so rightly demonstrate, assessment can be, and indeed should be, so much more than a simple measurement device. It can be a vital component of the therapeutic process. This book helps you to access the potential benefits of assessment and to avoid its possible downsides.

Furthermore, assessment is likely to be more effective if it is an ongoing process. This means that it should be an infinitely variable activity, one that should be tailored to fit the needs of each individual client. One extremely important contribution that this book makes to our understanding of the inherent complexity of assessment is the carefully drawn distinction between private practice assessors and assessors working for organisations or agencies. The differences between these sectors will, of course, tend to underpin differences in assessment style and practice. This book does an invaluable job in encouraging us to properly think about all the issues and their effects on our therapeutic practices.

Understanding Assessment in Counselling and Psychotherapy is essential reading for both experienced and developing practitioners/assessors alike.

Dr Norman Claringbull
Series editor
www.normanclaringbull.co.uk

Acknowledgements

Sofie Bager-Charleson: I would like to thank Biljana for instigating this project. It was her idea to write a book about assessment and it has been both a pleasure and a privilege to collaborate with her again. I am also grateful to colleagues and friends within both the Metanoia Institute and the Surrey Counselling and Psychotherapy Initiative (SCPI) for their inspiration and valuable feedback. Finally, I want to thank my family: my ever-supportive husband Dermot, our inspiring children Fina, Finbar and Leo, and my 'fellow-writer' and mother, Anna-Lena Bager. As always, you bring meaning and purpose to everything I do.

Biljana van Rijn: I would like to thank Metanoia Institute and the assessors who took part in the research project presented in the book and contributed so much to the development of the assessment training programme; my co-author Sofie, for being my 'critical friend' and her reflexivity and kindness; and the editorial team at Learning Matters for their patience.

About the authors

Sofie Bager-Charleson is a UKCP and BACP accredited psychotherapist and holds a PhD from Lund University, Sweden, where she specialised in parental involvements and the reflective practice of teachers within education. Sofie has also trained as a therapist within Relate and at Roehampton University, where she conducted research in reflective practice in counselling and psychotherapy. She is currently working as an academic supervisor at the Metanoia Institute on its joint doctorate programme with Middlesex University.

Dr Biljana van Rijn is Head of Clinical Services at the Metanoia Institute in London, where she has developed assessment training and a research clinic. She teaches on the MSc programme in Transactional Analysis Psychotherapy and is a research tutor and supervisor on the Doctorate in Counselling Psychology and Integrative Psychotherapy. Biljana also works as a psychotherapist and supervisor in a private practice in West Sussex.

Introduction

THE PURPOSE AND LAYOUT OF THE BOOK

This book is divided into two sections, which are basically two sides to the same story, each revolving around clients turning to counsellors and psychotherapists for help with living. Most of us are likely to regard this kind of encounter as a humbling experience. Many of us have made this move ourselves at some point and can recall the sense of bewilderment and vulnerability involved in the initial point of contact. Many people seek therapy with an acute sense of 'pain' that cannot be talked about in the same way that we address a broken leg or a twisted ankle. This adds to the confusion. Something is hurting and, at times, has a paralysing effect. The hurt is very much 'there' in the person's life; it is present yet escapes our efforts to capture, define and 'do' something about it.

Assessment is usually the first step in this rather esoteric process. It is the pathway to a unique reflective journey, where uncertainties are not only tolerated but welcomed as means of matching the ambiguity of life itself. We do not know how life 'ought' to be lived; no one knows the secret of living. What therapy *can* offer, however, is the strength and trust to tolerate this ambiguity. It can also help people to approach life with a renewed sense of direction based on authenticity and personal points of reference rather than guidance from others, for instance, parents, carers or maybe from socio-cultural expectations.

The first section approaches this humbling encounter between a client and a therapist in the context of private practice, at home or maybe in a rented room. The other section explores the same kind of meeting but in the context of an agency or organisation. The two sections also illustrate some variations and differences in therapists' outlook and focus. Like all therapists, my co-author, Biljana, and I 'see' things differently, both inside and outside our consulting rooms. The way assessment is presented in this book in the first place is invariably influenced by the way we select and interpret information. In our writing, values and beliefs seep into our respective 'stories'. We are – be it as writers, researchers or therapists – 'co-constituting' the outcome. As the term 'reflexivity' implies, we engage with the information and become *a central figure who actively constructs the collection, selection and interpretation* (Finlay and Gough, 2003, p5). Meanings are, in this sense, always negotiated within particular contexts, and another writer or researcher would invariably, as Finlay puts it, *unfold a different story*.

As a means of reflecting over how we have gathered and interpreted information or what, in reflective practice, is referred to as having 'framed' situations, we both attempt to be as transparent about ourselves and our 'blind spots' as we can. Before we start to tackle the concept of assessment, we would like to tell you something about the personal, cultural and theoretical 'biases' and underlying assumptions that affect our understanding(s) – we will introduce ourselves to you in what we call our personal 'stories'.

SOFIE'S STORY

Biases, potential blind spots and 'shadows' are aspects that I have referred to earlier in writings (Bager-Charleson, 2010a, 2010b). To avoid going over old ground, I will refer to my background more briefly here.

I grew up in a household with a bipolar parent. I believe that this had a huge impact on me and my subsequent outlook on life. Being a child of a bipolar parent gives 'framings' and the way we make sense of things a very tangible meaning. The fact that there are different understandings of the 'same' reality affects all aspects of life – from how to get dressed in the mornings to what political party to support and why. As therapists, we are all likely to have our particular 'Achilles heel' or, as Jung (cited in Sedgwick, 1994, p15) would say, different types of *woundedness* or *shadow*. I believe that the need to negotiate between different and shifting outlooks has stayed with me.

My own personal therapy has been instrumental in helping me to draw on experiences out of choice, rather than submitting to what Winnicott (1965, p147) refers to as a *false self* where behaviours freeze in *compliance with environmental demands*. The idea of choice is something of which I need constant reminding, and my propensity for 'compulsive caring' makes me susceptible to colluding with clients who may think of themselves as helpless. There is nothing wrong in being wounded, but Jung warned us against enacting it or projecting our own issues on to the client. My own difficulties in this area have, over time, resulted in my interest in countertransference-related issues. Why we react as we do intrigues me, and the issue of why we work as therapists in the first place seems far from clear-cut from where I come from.

Ongoing conversations with colleagues, students and supervisees have convinced me that I am not alone in this kind of thinking. In fact, as we shall see later on, in a study (Bager-Charleson, 2010b) about why therapists choose to become therapists, the majority of those studied referred to either their own childhood or a crisis experienced as an adult as factors affecting their choice of career as counsellors or psychotherapists.

Theoretically, I anchor my practice in psychodynamic thinking. The idea of a presenting past has made particular sense to me. My own personal therapy has been psychoanalytically based, and I regard the seven years of therapy as time well spent. My personal therapy is probably what influences my own practice most. Just as in parenting, our own experiences of relationships are often drawn upon in moments when 'thinking on one's feet' is called for, for good and for bad. My integrative training at Roehampton University resonated with my ideas about different frameworks. The training involved studies in psychoanalytic, existential and postmodern theory, and my eventual theoretical outlook rests on the belief that there are different sides to each story. To my mind, therapy ultimately becomes a space and a place where we may, as Bion (1962) suggested, *learn to think for ourselves*. Like many contemporary therapists I disagree with the idea that we enter the consulting room as 'sterile surgeons'. I do not think it possible to provide our clients with an unpolluted space and free-range thought. Each client and therapist encounter becomes, in a sense, what Jung refers to in terms of the *alchemic concept* (Jung, cited in Sedgwick, 1994, p13), where they jointly, so to speak, make 'gold'. The dialectical nature of a meeting between two different people on this level can, suggests Jung, be compared with *combining two chemical substances* where *each has his or her respective conscious and unconscious parts, which in turn pull on each other* (Sedgwick, 1994, p13).

I grew up in Sweden during the 1960 and 1970s when its welfare model was at its strongest. In the early 1990s I moved to Spain and then England, which certainly impacted on the way I looked at identity. Life in Spain and England immersed me in new ways of thinking about life and prompted me to revisit, with new 'lenses', my ideas about ourselves in the world. Living in different cultures threw light on how so-called 'truths' are often based on values, beliefs and norms rather than facts. I agree with both constructivist and social constructionist thinking that as part of the 'alchemic' process we construct reality in response to both personal factors and our surrounding culture. When we meet another person, particularly for the first time, cultural expectations often dominate, and, as White (2006, p206) puts it, *social, sexual, racial and cultural differences [become] an integral part of the [psychotherapeutic] process*. Ironically, I recall an assessment with my first Swedish client as one of my most 'biased' sessions ever. I experienced the assessment session as a complete communication breakdown. It was only afterwards, in supervision, that I could see how I had expected the Swedish client to think and feel like me. It was also at this time that it occurred to me that meeting someone as a 'foreigner' in the sense that I invariably do with my British clients is often quite an appropriate approach regardless of origins.

The drive to understand a world filled with different understandings has brought me to different places and into many important relationships. Biljana is an example of a friend with whom I share the experience of different cultures and countries. Our common platforms combined with differences in our theoretical frameworks for practice make good ground for being 'critical friends'. Critical friends have really nothing to do with being critical. The term refers rather to a relationship into which you can put trust in each other to see things from your angle while adding a 'mirror' to potential blind spots – a relationship that has felt valuable to both of us when writing a book.

Our common platform is the concept of reflective practice. We are, for different reasons, passionate about this subject and have developed a professional practice around it. We hope that you will share our interest in reflective practice. But the ultimate aim is to provide you with a book that you can enjoy and that enables you to feel free to select, collect and interpret the information we provide in a way that will benefit both you and your clients.

BILJANA'S STORY

I have always been interested in how people give meaning to their experiences and what has contributed to them. This influenced my choice of theoretical orientation in psychotherapy. Transactional analysis (TA) places a particular emphasis on the narratives and stories people create in their lives. Eric Berne, the founder of TA, coined the term 'life script' and defined it as a *life plan based on a decision made in childhood, reinforced by the parents, justified by subsequent events, and culminating in a chosen alternative* (Berne, 1972, p445). This concept suggests that we initially create our stories based on our early experiences, then continue to interact with the world in such a way that it repeats our early beliefs. Our early narratives are not conscious, but they are predictable and may seem to be a 'life plan'. The aim of transactional analysis psychotherapy is to make people aware of their 'life scripts', increase their choices and help them develop new narratives. The relational transactional analysis I draw on in my work *has been represented by a move away from the focus on cognitive insight as the primary means of psychological change, to the importance of effective, co-creative, conscious, non-conscious and unconscious relational interactions as a primary means of growth, change and transformation* (International Association of Relational Transactional Analysis; see **www relationalta.com**). Relational transactional analysis embraces a two-person psychology and draws on postmodern philosophies. This has helped me to use it to frame my own experiences.

Living and working in a different country, and in a different language, has helped me to understand both the importance of culture in how people create their inner worlds and my desire to create a bridge between my different cultural experiences.

This book is one such bridge, a bridge between clinical work and organisations. Clinicians need to use their therapeutic skills to meet and assess clients, while working in the context of an organisation. This requires skill and a willingness to engage with both client and organisation. An assessor who is isolated from the organisation in which they work and applies counselling principles without a dynamic relationship to their context may not be offering the best service to their clients. For example, how can a counsellor working in a GP practice ensure their client's confidentiality while having a medical back-up and working as a member of a team?

The idea for a book on assessments in organisations emerged from my long-standing involvement with clinical assessments at the Metanoia Counselling and Psychotherapy Service (MCPS) where I work as the Head of Clinical Services. MCPS offers medium-term counselling and psychotherapy with trainee practitioners. The Metanoia Institute is a relational psychotherapy and counselling training institute, which has reflective practice at the core of its training.

Initially, as an experienced psychotherapist, I conducted all the assessments by telephone. As the service developed and had more resources I trained and supervised assessors who conducted assessments face to face with clients and engaged in training and supervision with me. Using the principles of reflective practice, the first group of assessors and I conducted a collaborative action enquiry into the process of developing assessment skills and focused on the training needs of assessors within the organisation. The findings of the enquiry were used to develop a structured assessment and training model within the organisation, and form the basis of Chapters 5 and 6.

ASSESSMENT IN PRIVATE PRACTICE

Chapter 1 looks at some characteristics specific to private practice, with concepts such as self-knowledge, networks, professionalism and safety in mind. Assessment is viewed in the context of a 'two-person' psychology, with an emphasis on the collaborative, interactive nature of therapeutic practice. This perspective encourages us to take the therapist's own impact on problems into consideration when assessing. Reflective practice, reflexivity and ethical guidelines are introduced as points of reference when securing ongoing feedback and support for the therapist. The term 'double-loop' assessment is used as a reminder of the importance of being open to new and different perspectives. Reflexivity is a term that refers to 'looping back' or returning to a problem with a focus on different and sometimes 'foreign' angles. On what do we base our ideas about what is good, bad, sane, insane, normal and not normal? Why do we find some people suitable for therapy and others not? Psychotherapeutic practice is not a clear-cut science, and this is reflected in the assessment process. As Jenkins (2007, p6) puts it, therapeutic practice does not follow the *adversarial proceedings* of law where *one side wins and the other loses, through a robust process of proving and disproving*. Rather, it is about prizing the raw, subjective nature of individual experience and working with ambiguity and metaphor rather than literal truth. In Chapter 1 the meaning of 'doing no harm' and the issues surrounding referrals, contracts and problems, such as how to assess the client's 'readiness' for therapy, will be explored with regard to truth, right and wrong in mind.

Chapter 2 tackles the issue of formulating a hypothesis and aiming for a diagnosis of the problem with a strategy for further therapy. The chapter takes a closer look at the difference between diagnosis and formulation. We will explore different 'strands' (Holmes, 1995) of the first interview in terms of understanding both 'with' and 'about' the client. The concept of diagnosis is used for the process of 'sieving' for themes during assessment, and different kinds of themes are reflected upon in case studies. 'Sieving' information is considered in the context of evidence-based and practice-based practice (Barkham et al., 2010). 'Sieving' is also explored in the light of hypothesising and, as Hinshelwood (1995, p156) puts it, something to 'try out' with the client with evidence resting on the client's response. We will also look at the difficulties involved in 'practising what we preach' by exploring what Argyris and Schön (1978; Bager-Charleson 2010a) coined as a conflict between an 'espoused' theory and a theory-in-use. Safety and referrals are explored further in the light of ethical guidelines and sometimes conflicting interests.

Chapter 3 analyses how different modalities approach 'problems'. What can we offer in private practice with regard to 'treatment'? We will pursue Hinshelwood's (1995) thinking on hypotheses as an ongoing attempt to put out 'markers' as means of *recognising the currents in the interaction that pull or push* the therapist. The issue of 'markers' will be compared between the core modalities. What are the differences and similarities between the different models? What guides the therapist and the client through the different types of therapeutic processes or journeys? We will return to the issue of the therapist as a person with case studies that revisit key themes for this section, such as countertransference, double-loop thinking and ethical guidelines.

ASSESSMENT IN ORGANISATIONS

There are many overlaps between assessments in private practice and those in organisations. I will revisit some of the core concepts, which Sofie covers in more depth at the beginning of the book, and focus on some of the organisational perspectives in relation to them.

Chapter 4 gives an overview of different organisations that offer counselling and psychotherapy on an outpatient basis and different methods of assessment. Inpatient treatments in hospitals and therapeutic communities are outside the remit of this book. This chapter will give an overview of the skills used within the two assessment methods: assessment by telephone and assessment by face-to-face interview. Chapters 5 and 6 focus on the detail of assessment in organisations. Many of them will be relevant in other settings and provide an additional area for reflection in both private practice and organisations.

As well as using theoretical sources and literature I present the experiential knowledge gained through the collaborative reflective enquiry (Heron and Reason, 2001) into the assessment processes and skills in which I engaged in 2006 and 2007, with a group of trainee assessors at the Metanoia Counselling and Psychotherapy Service (MCPS). We used supervision sessions to analyse the assessment process and identify training needs for students. This was then used to develop an assessment training programme at the Metanoia Institute that I still run. Transcripts from these sessions have been used, in both Chapters 5 and 6, to illustrate concepts and give examples. All assessors have agreed to this use of transcripts.

Chapter 5 presents broad assessment processes and strategies in organisations where the assessor has a responsibility to make a decision whether or not to accept a client for treatment. In this type of setting the assessor does not offer treatment or have an ongoing relationship with a client. This approach is common in both statutory and non-statutory organisations, has a particular dynamic and challenges, and requires some specialised skills. The organisational setting is unlike the private practice setting in that the assessor is bound by organisational policies and has an organisational role, and resources are limited by the organisation.

Chapter 6 focuses on specific assessment skills and outcomes of the assessment. It also offers a chance to reflect on the complexity of the assessor's role in this setting and the impact on the assessor as a person.

CHAPTER 1

The role of the assessor in private practice

> **CORE KNOWLEDGE**
> - Our first encounters with clients will be explored in the context of ethical and morally binding guidelines for assessment. We will explore the meaning of 'doing no harm' and the aim of setting realistic targets.
> - What do we think of when seeing clients alone in our homes? This chapter will look at expectations, contracts and the importance of mutual consent.
> - How do we assess 'readiness' for therapy? Is therapy always the answer? If not, what happens next? We will look at the importance of respecting the clients' defences and consider if and when a client may be likely to benefit from other forms of support.
> - The only 'tool' that the therapist brings into the room is themselves, which makes self-awareness such an important part of clinical practice. The term 'double-loop assessment' is introduced to help us understand how we can develop a 'reflexive awareness' in our practice. Reflexive awareness involves considering how our own underlying personal theoretical and cultural assumptions can affect assessment.

INTRODUCTION

As counsellors and psychotherapists we are expected to notice many things on different levels. Each encounter with a new client is full of competing impressions. Body language, clothing, tone of voice and facial expressions can be as important to a client's story as their actual verbal account of events. The case study below highlights how our first meeting with a client involves a multitude of messages.

Case study 1.1

There is the sound of a faint cough outside the door.

'Hmm, have I got the right house?' asks the man, as the therapist opens the door.

'Mr Mott?'

The short, rather stocky man in his mid-thirties nods in reply and continues talking while entering the room.

'Have any of your clients ever gone into the wrong building by mistake?' he chuckles.

'Have a seat . . .'

'Anyway, yes, I am Mr Mott. Call me Jack, by all means.'

Jack is wearing a suit and keeps flicking at some invisible dust on his left thigh. He looks well attended to, with a crisp white shirt and a tie. He sits with his legs wide apart. As he opens his mouth to speak again, tears begin to roll down his cheeks. He looks out of the window and speaks fast, while crying as if the tears have got nothing to do with him – as if they are not there.

'As I said on the phone, I've got a couple of issues at work that I'd like to discuss. There's been a promotion . . . and, well, I'm also thinking about getting married. It's the second time around. My first wife attacked me with her high-heeled shoes on our wedding night, so I'd rather avoid going down that route again!' He chuckles through his tears.

At this stage, the therapist decides to . . .

COMMENT

What would *you* do at this stage? Would you, for instance, choose to let Jack develop his narratives further, uninterrupted – perhaps hoping to gain information that way about how Jack deals with new situations and people? Or would this be a good moment to change tack and maybe bring out an assessment sheet or address some standard questions, perhaps with a view to considering mutual aims and objectives at the earliest possible stage?

Or is it perhaps likely that a different scenario would have emerged, had you been at the door to meet Jack? Some therapists start their first interview with an assessment questionnaire. Others aim for things to develop more 'organically'. Some may argue that a relatively unstructured beginning allows valuable information about the client's way of relating to new situations to be revealed. The way clients choose to address issues such as personal problems, work and relationships may help the therapist gauge how the client relates to priorities and how they organise their lives. Others would argue that this kind of information will come out anyway, and that the first interview is primarily concerned with addressing aims and objectives, reaching a mutual consent and being transparent.

The way we approach our clients varies depending on our modality, personality and general approach to practice. It also varies depending on the setting in which we work. The case study above was written with a middle-aged female private practitioner with a psychodynamic background in mind. It is possible that meeting a middle-aged woman has a particular significance for the client. Perhaps the first moments of the meeting would have developed differently if the therapist had been a thirty-year-old male? Factors such as age, gender, ethnicity and social background affect practice in different ways – not only in the way that the practitioner might pay attention to, and interpret, information but also in the way the client will react. The first impression is important for both parties. Green asserts:

> *As a counsellor you need to give considerable thought to the client's perception of you and how it might impact upon the work . . .*
> (Green, 2010, p16)

Regular supervision and personal therapy will help us to explore and monitor what we, as therapists, bring into the sessions. This book is written with that kind of self-awareness in mind. We hope that you will read the book from the perspective of both yourself and your clients, and with consideration to some of the following questions.

- What are you looking for in your first meeting with clients? Why?
- What are your clients likely to encounter (see, hear, feel) during their first interview with you, in your particular practice? Why?

DO WE NEED ASSESSMENT IN PRIVATE PRACTICE?

Working independently and separately from agencies and organisations brings a degree of flexibility. Certainly, private practice can, as Withers (2007, p52) puts it, *offer a highly targeted and confidential service tailored to the specific choices, details and dilemmas with which each client presents*. Some would argue that there is less need for assessment in private practice in light of the fact that both therapist and client are often prepared for moving straight on to therapy, provided that mutual terms can be negotiated. Withers writes:

> *It could be argued that there is no need for assessment in private practice as, unlike statutory or agency work, the therapist tends to be assessing those clients whom he or she will continue to see.*
> (2007, p53)

FINANCIAL DYNAMICS

Yet, continues Withers, assessment is inevitable. Any new social encounter involves a mutual scrutiny, and a first encounter in private practice is obviously no different. The notion of choice in private practice can, in fact, as Withers (2007, p50) suggests, involve *far greater challenges than those posed for the therapist working within a statutory service*. Withers refers to *financial dynamics*:

> *For the therapist, decisions made via the assessment process may look as if they are based solely on experienced clinical judgement. However, it is inevitable that the fundamental financial dynamics at the heart of private practice suggest that these will contain unconscious invitations to collude and anxieties about much they can be confronted . . . [O]ur client has actual purchasing power with attendant ability to shop around – and crucially to assess not just trustworthiness but desirability of the therapist as partner in the whole enterprise.*
>
> (2007, pp52, 50)

LIABILITY

Linked to what Withers refers to as his *shadows* of the freedom to be *vulnerable to mutually seductive and even delusional thinking* about what the therapist can offer is the issue of liability in case of client disappointment. It is important, asserts Jenkins (2007), for therapists to be familiar with the difference between *personal* and *vicarious* liability. Employers have got a common law duty to protect employees. Jenkins writes:

> *Employment relationships are key factors in deciding where liability for negligence lies. Where a therapist is employed, or working as if employed by [for instance a] GP practice, then the practice would hold vicarious liability for any mistakes or poor practice. Where the therapist is self-employed . . . then the therapist would be liable for any action brought by a dissatisfied client.*
>
> (2007, p35)

There are, in other words, both practical issues and arbitrary concerns that rear their heads in private practice. On what basis do I reach consent and form contracts with my clients? How do I frame my decisions ethically, professionally and personally? What happens if the client is disappointed with the outcome? How can good practice and safety for both clients and the therapist be catered for, when we work in isolation, often from home?

THE DOUBLE-LOOP ASSESSOR – ASSESSING OUTSIDE THE BOX

As the Jungian analyst Guggenbühl-Craig (2009) points out, the only actual 'tool' that the therapist brings into the room is themselves. In the light of this, Guggenbühl-Craig stresses the importance of honesty and self-awareness:

> *We work with our own psyche, our own person, without instruments, methods of technology. Our tools are ourselves, our honesty, our own personal contact with the unconscious and the irrational . . .*
> (2009, p73)

In private practice we are often free to choose peers and supervisors. The invaluable input from others can sometimes be reduced to feedback from a group of people who think and feel like ourselves.

ACTIVITY 1.1

The term 'critical friend' is a concept often used in reflective practice. Beverly Taylor defines 'critical friend' thus:

> *A critical friend . . . is someone you trust and respect . . . [and who] can offer external perspective to extend your reflective capacity.*
> (Taylor, 2006, p64)

- Take some time to think about who you could consider as a critical friend.

Reflective practice is based on the belief that there is always a risk that we become too comfortable and miss out on the valuable option of conflicting views and broadening perspectives. Reflective practice is often referred to in professions involving people, such as social work, teaching, nursing and psychotherapy. Reflective practice (Schön, 1983; Schön and Rein, 1994; Bolton, 2005; White et al., 2008; Bager-Charleson, 2010a) is an ongoing concern and a strategy to be applied throughout our clinical practice. It encourages us to develop and nourish a *reflexive awareness* (Parker 1994, 2004; Alvesson and Skoldeberg, 2000; Finlay and Gough, 2003; Etherington, 2004) about what impact our own underlying personal, theoretical and cultural assumptions may have on the problem. Fiona Gardner proposes:

> *[Reflective practice] is an approach in which the learner is encouraged to be as reflexively aware as possible of their social, political and psychological position, and to question it, as well as their environment.*
> (Gardner, 2008, pp156–72)

Reflective practice seeps, naturally, into assessment. In this context, assessment will be explored with particular reference to what Donald Schön, the founder of reflective practice, coined as *double-loop learning*. We will use a model (see Figure 1.1 on page 18) from our previous book about reflective practice (Bager-Charleson, 2010a) to illustrate what we mean by reflexive awareness.

Reflective practice involves a contract between client and therapist that reflects ethical thinking about autonomy, i.e. where the client understands the nature of therapy and what to expect. Reflective practice is based on being open to unique and different perspectives instead of holding on to a standardised 'expert stance' approach to problem solving.

TWO-PERSON PSYCHOLOGIES

Many writers (Schön, 1983; Sussman, 1992; Sedgwick, 1994; Page, 1999; Withers, 2007) warn us against the 'expert' helper who thinks that they have got all the answers. Withers alerts us to *sterile and collusive experiences* as an outcome of adopting an objective expert stance to the assessment process:

> *If therapists insist that the assessment interview is a wholly objective process, there are two major pits into which they are likely to fall. One is to close down too early all the multiple possibilities in the client's narrative for the sake of therapeutic consistency and the other is to deny their own involvement and need.*
>
> (2007, p66)

There is, as Safran and Muran (2003, p13) put it, a cultural shift towards a *postmodern sensibility*, which *challenges the traditional view that the therapist can have some privileged understanding of reality*.

KEY CONCEPTS   Postmodernism

Safran and Muran (2003) mention *a cultural shift towards a postmodern sensibility* where the idea of experts with privileged understanding of reality comes under scrutiny. Rather than assuming that therapists and *psychologists merely adapt to social demands*, Kvale (1999, p43) and other postmodernist thinkers highlight how therapists in fact also *shape* social demands. Kvale asserts that *the science of psychology has also contributed to the shaping of the current culture* (1999, p43).

Together with psychiatrists and psychologists, psychotherapists are often instrumental in sustaining beliefs about sanity, normality, good and bad.

continued overleaf

> However, as Loewenthal and Snell (2003) put it, assessments are, like everything else, *subject to* values and beliefs. Ideas about sanity and normality are never static or completely neutral. Kvale (1999, p32) refers to postmodernism as *characterised by a loss of belief in an objective world*. It reflects a reaction against the industrialised, modern society with its idea of universal 'truths' and objective, verifiable rights and wrongs. Postmodern thinkers highlight how culture and language shapes us, which Loewenthal and Snell assert is essential to consider in psychotherapy. Postmodern theory is a *plea for humility* and a *challenge to omnipotence*. All types of assessment are *subject to* circumstances and need to be understood in the context of language, power and cultural differences:
>
>> *The post-modern shift in European thinking reflects values and attitudes which are important for any therapeutic practice . . . For example, to respond more appropriately to the world from which patients/clients come . . . Post-modern Continental philosophers suggest that we are 'subject to' . . . By reminding that we are subjects-to(o), it can a challenge to omnipotence, both the patient's and the therapist's, and can be a plea for humility . . . It questions whether language and speech ever is neutral. It can alert us that language is never static . . . [we are always] subject to language . . . to the other and to difference . . . to power/knowledge relationships . . . and the constant deferral of meaning.*
>>
>> (2003, p1)

Clinical knowledge naturally plays a crucial role in assessment and ongoing therapy. But if the classical one-person psychologies based on the therapist as a blank screen or a sterile surgeon is gradually being replaced by a more egalitarian, transparent, collaborative 'two-person' model, our idea of assessment changes too. Safran and Muran write:

> *In a two-person psychology, the patient-therapist relationship is the object of study, and the therapist is considered a co-participant rather than one who stands outside . . . [This] suggests that clinical formulations must always be guided by and revised in light of information gleaned from an ongoing exploration of what is taking place in the here-and-now of the therapeutic relationship.*
>
> (2003, p39)

The concept of 'formulation' that Safran and Muran use above is often used to highlight a distance from 'diagnosis', which can carry unrealistic expectations of medical expertise. We will return to the concept in the next chapter when we discuss 'diagnosing'. In brief, formulation emphasises the tentative, ongoing and collaborative nature that assessments may have, without losing sight of the importance of adopting a focus for the work. An expressed focus is needed to 'formulate' a shared understanding and reach an informed consent about what the therapeutic process will entail. As we shall see further on in this section, this initial agreement is essential for *good practice*; it is the basis of what, in ethical terms, is referred to as *autonomy* (Jenkins, 2007, p10), which involves an *informed consent* where the client has understood the nature of therapy and what to expect. An initial agreement about a tentative focus is equally important for the therapist and their *duty to work to the relevant standards set for the profession*. A *competent assessment*, then, is a way to consider whether the therapist is sufficiently trained, qualified and skilled in order to practise safely and to provide the appropriate level of care to the client (Jenkins, 2007, p10).

> ### REFLECTION POINT
>
> - How do you see your role as a therapist?
> - Consider what you are *certain* that you can contribute as a therapist. Then consider the things that you *hope* to achieve as a therapist. Was it difficult or easy to come up with certainties?

THE THERAPIST'S EMOTIONS

The classical one-person psychologies referred to earlier require an objective expert who is capable of leaving their emotions outside the room. It was the idea of leaving emotions to one side that inspired Freud to coin the phrase 'countertransference'. Within the one-person psychologies the therapist's own emotional responses were – and, indeed, still are – either unwanted and in need of elimination through further analysis or something that belonged to the client but had been projected upon the therapist. On the other hand, two-person psychologies suggest that the therapist *has an inescapable, inextricable involvement in all that goes on in the interview* and that countertransference is a natural expression of the therapist's own emotions (Safran and Muran, 2003, p39).

> ### KEY CONCEPTS   Countertransference
>
> As mentioned above, Freud's initial stance was that analysts themselves should aim to eradicate their own emotional responses through personal therapy. However, as Alberts (1998, p99) says, *later writers modify Freud's position. They recognised that . . . it is unrealistic to expect a therapist to*
>
> *continued overleaf*

> *remain completely neutral.* Indeed, as Rabinowitz puts it: *The good therapist has got reasons to be proud of his ability to feel and know what he is feeling* (1998, xv).
>
> Countertransference is a term that is used today within psychoanalytic and psychodynamic theory to relate to the therapist's emotions in a broader sense.
>
> Holmes and Lindley (1998) refer to countertransference as something that deals with both:
>
> - the therapist's 'blind spots', i.e. 'unconscious' reactions involving wishes and fantasies in relation to the client; and
> - effective responses to the client, which we as therapists are aware of and think can be of good use in helping us to better understand the client.

REFLECTION POINT

- Can you think of situations – either in practice or in a role play – where you have experienced strong emotions with a client?
- If so, who do you feel that the strong emotions belonged to? From where did they originate?

'THEORETICAL' COUNTERTRANSFERENCE

In addition to the influence of the therapist's emotional 'baggage', O'Hanlon and Bertolino have coined the concept of 'theoretical countertransference' to highlight how our choice of clinical model can influence our understanding of the problem. Hemmings and Field write:

> *It is . . . important to recognise that a counsellor who is absolutely 'certain' is one to be avoided as they may fall into the Procrustean trap of attempting to fit their client into their theory instead of listening. O'Hanlon and Bertolino (1998) refer to this as 'theoretical countertransference'.*
>
> (2007, p147)

As Gergen (cited in Rosen and Kuehlwein 1996, p21) puts it, any theoretical view both sensitises and constrains, so that *one sees more sharply but remains blind to that which falls outside the realm of focus.*

THE SOCIAL ROLE(S) OF THE ASSESSOR

Milner and O'Byrne (2004) argue that therapy is a political concern, and that our practice conveys norms and values that can be linked to a bigger cultural, political context. We contribute in order to make society 'work' and run smoothly. An example of an underlying cultural assumption is that a child should attend school. Do we ultimately, ask Milner and O'Byrne, assess 'needs' with the interest of our client or society in mind? They contend that counsellors *are political agents, however much they may disavow this* (2004, p17).

One of the cornerstones in reflective practice is that there are always alternative ways of framing problems (Schön, 1983). Wen-Shing Tseng and Streltzer agree with the political angle to our roles as therapists. They too stress the importance of considering the impact that our social values and sometimes unacknowledged biases can have on how we assess the client's 'problem':

> *The process of mental assessment is coloured by the cultural backgrounds of both the patient and the clinician to the extent that it may confuse or bias the assessment . . . The clinical picture is influenced by many factors, such as . . . age, gender, educational background as well as ethnic-cultural factors.*
>
> (1997, p27)

Cultural biases may be one of the most difficult – if not sometimes impossible – aspects to grasp and understand. We are immersed in values and beliefs; we live them, breathe them, they surround us from the moment that we are born. As mentioned earlier, I had expected it to be 'easier' to relate to Swedish clients and welcomed the first Swedish-speaking client who contacted me when I first set up my practice in the UK. Our initial lack of connection came as a surprise to both of us. I felt 'stuck' right from the start. My supervisor helped me to recognise that not only had I assumed that I would understand my client's way of thinking, I had also expected her to share my outlook and possibly even life goals. I was, in other words, unable to hear her side of the story or, as Lacan suggests, unable to travel on her side of the carriage and see the world from her unique perspective. To illustrate that there is no unequivocal meaning, Lacan relates the following story:

> *A train arrives at a station. A brother and sister are seated in a compartment face-to-face next to the window. As the train pulls to a stop: 'Look', says the brother, 'We're at Ladies!' 'Idiot!' replies his sister, 'Can't you see we're at Gentlemen'.*
>
> (Lacan in Sarup, 1993, p11)

THE ROLE OF THE ASSESSOR IN PRIVATE PRACTICE

The experience with my Swedish client brought home to me how biases and sometimes prejudices can seep into the room in many different ways. With this in mind, Milner and O'Byrne propose that one of the greatest obstacles for good practice is unintentional abuse of power. Milner and O'Byrne write:

> *Whilst we cannot legislate for the unprincipled counsellor, we can look at the ways in which we may unintentionally abuse the power we hold in the therapeutic relationship.*
>
> (2004, p19)

REFLECTION POINT

- Can you think of any situations where you have unintentionally 'abused' your power in the therapeutic relationship, for example, with reference to gender, ethnicity or social class?

Reflective practice is all about these kinds of implicit and often unintentionally biased ways of reaching conclusions. To facilitate this thinking about blind spots and biases, we have used the idea of a double-loop assessment (see Figure 1.1).

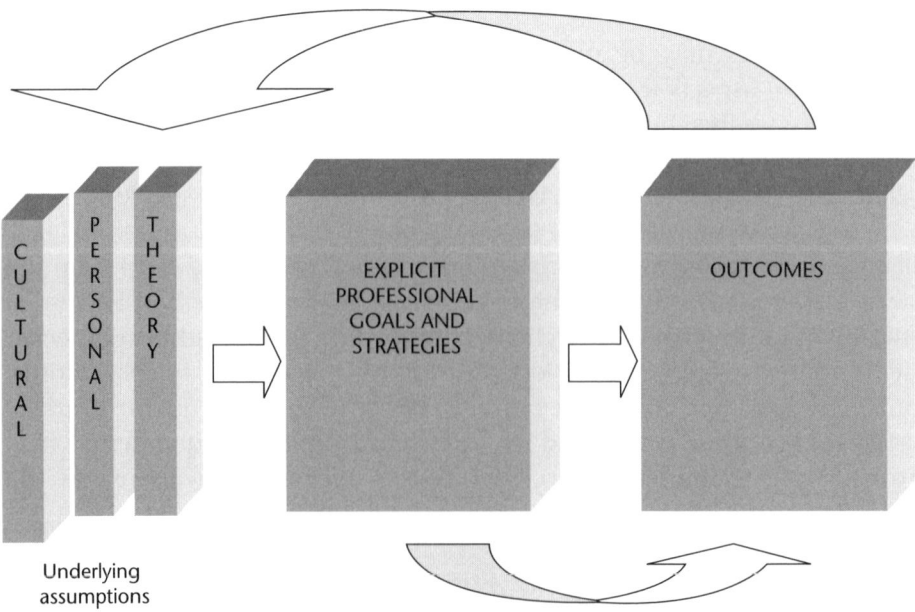

Figure 1.1: Double-loop learning to expand the analytical frame beyond 'the obvious', to explicitly identify and challenge underlying cultural, personal and theoretical assumptions

> **REFLECTION POINT**
>
> Reflective assessment with double-loop learning encourages us to consider two questions.
>
> - How do my underlying personal, cultural and/or theoretical beliefs and assumptions affect the assessment?
> - What do I need in terms of personal and professional support to develop new and alternative perspectives?

The double loop refers to an extra loop of analysis when exploring problems. This loop is usually triggered by the sense that something is wrong, for instance, when clients fail to turn up as agreed, 'always' stay ten minutes over time or regularly forget to bring money to pay for their session. The double loop encourages us to consider our own contribution to the matter. To do so, therapists sometimes need as much support as clients to deal with stubborn patterns of behaviour and resistance to change. Our first reaction when confronting our own biases and patterns of behaviour can range from sadness to denial. But to work within the ethical framework suggested earlier, we need to explore our own understandings in light of other new and different ways of being. The double loop can sometimes happen through our own reflections or it can be nourished by supervision, personal therapy, peer groups or further reading and training. Adopting and 'trying on' new and 'foreign' lenses invariably brings new perspectives to the way we frame and structure our understanding of problems.

SUPERVISION

Supervision is an important requirement for reflective practice. Counsellors and psychotherapists are expected to undertake a minimum of 1.5 hours of supervision per month. Supervision and peer groups contribute ongoing invaluable support in terms of clinical, ethical and emotional feedback. Proctor (1986) suggests that we expect support in three areas from our supervision. She refers to our ethical, educational and personal needs in terms of 'normative', 'formative' and 'restorative', and encourages us to ask questions such as the following.

- How are my normative needs met? How do I safeguard support with regard to professional and ethical guidelines, norms and laws?
- What are my formative needs? Do I safeguard the support that I need to develop skills, theoretical knowledge and personal attributes as a practitioner?

- How are my restorative needs catered for? Do I feel listened to, supported and confronted with regard to my personal issues, needs and insecurities?

> **ACTIVITY 1.2**
>
> - Take some time to note down to what extent your own needs are met in supervision.

ETHICAL GUIDELINES

As yet, 'registered medical practitioner', 'chartered psychologist' and 'registered nurse' are the only occupational terms that have legal restrictions on their current use. Jenkins (2007, pp5, 6) writes that the terms 'counsellor', 'therapist' and 'psychotherapist' as self-defined occupational terms have as yet no legal restrictions on their use, and he concludes that in the absence of legal restrictions, ethical guidelines become paramount. Ethics provide us with a framework for what is *morally* right or wrong, rather than resting on the *robust process of proving and disproving*, which signifies the 'adversarial proceedings' of the law. Ethical guidelines reflect the need for rules that take into account the fact that therapeutic practice rests on 'stories' and joint interpretations:

> *Therapy and the law operate within distinctly different discourses. Whereas therapeutic practice prizes the raw, subjective nature of individual experience, and works with ambiguity and metaphor rather than literal truth, the law is concerned with establishing objective, verifiable facts . . . where one side wins and the other loses, through a robust process of proving and disproving.*
>
> (Jenkins, 2007, p6)

Therapy and law, writes Jenkins (2007, p4), *enjoy, at best, an uneasy relationship*. There are different ethical decision-making models to help therapists with difficult events occurring both inside and outside the courtroom. The British Association for Counselling and Psychotherapy (BACP) offers an accessible and broad framework for ethical consideration (BACP, 2010). The BACP ethical framework is, as Gabriel and Casemore (2010, p1) put it, *based on professional obligation to provide adequate care and attention . . . in an ethically sound way*. This ethical framework is not law abiding as such, but it does require therapists to *develop a basic, working knowledge of the law* (Jenkins, 2007, p8). Therapists should *remain accountable for their decisions both in an ethical sense and in terms of the law*.

The relationship of the law to therapy is complex, continues Jenkins, but is mediated through three main factors. These are:

- the context or setting in which the therapist practises;
- the therapist's employment status in terms of being employed or self-employed; and
- the actual client group.

The BACP ethical framework (BACP, 2010) offers the following principles to hold on to in our assessment as well as in ongoing practice.

- *Fidelity and keeping to one's word* Can I do what I said I would do? Am I fit, able to keep to my word?
- *Autonomy and allowing clients make informed choices* When and how do I admit to own limits and restrictions?
- *Beneficence and duty to care* Am I qualified, appropriately trained and equipped for this particular client work?
- *Non-maleficence and 'never do harm'* How do I reach professional opinions and decisions? What harm can I cause directly or indirectly to clients?
- *Justice and treating clients fairly* Can I give all clients equal treatment, time and energy? How do I relate to cultural diversity, gender issues, disability etc?
- *Self-respect* Self-respect involves checking that you have applied all the ethical guidelines to yourself. Have you?

Fidelity

Fidelity is about being trustworthy and always trying to practise what we preach. Dale writes that *the ethical principle of fidelity is about willingly agreeing to do what you can . . . [therefore] be clear about your own boundaries* (2008, p3).

In private practice, our promises to clients sometimes begin through a website or in adverts in newspapers, magazines or *Yellow Pages*. The notion of choice can, as we will explore later, have a particular significance for both the client and the therapist in private practice. It is, for instance, tempting to 'stand out' in order to reach clients for our practice, but at the same time it is important not to promise anything that we cannot keep. Gabriel and Casemore (2010, p3) assert that being trustworthy *brings into question the person of the practitioner*. It assumes that the therapist can be relied upon with regard to *their personal and professional knowledge, skills and abilities, as well as their values and attitudes*.

Autonomy

This is about ensuring that the client agrees to further therapy on the basis of an informed decision. Autonomy is, as Gabriel and Casemore (2010, p3) put it, about making decisions and actions that *respect and maximise the opportunities for individuals to implement their own reasoned and informed choices*. Autonomy requires an ongoing sensitivity to the client's ability to locate themselves during the therapeutic process. It is, of course, in the first interview that the foundation is laid for the future relationship, and it is here that the egalitarian relationship is being introduced. One way of honouring the client's autonomy is to stick to *the twin principle of minimum intervention and not doing harm* (Aveline, 1997, p109). The principle of 'minimum intervention' is linked to the realistic assumption about counselling and psychotherapy as *aids to life, not solutions or substitutes*. Aveline continues:

> *The sooner therapy can enable the client to discover and use their strength the better . . . do the minimum necessary to enable movement to take place in a client's life . . . [T]he rule of thumb is to start with the most urgent need and work from the superficial to the deeper, more complex problems.*
> (1997, p109)

In the context of assessment, autonomy rests ultimately on whether the client can work with you on the basis of the information that you are able to provide. To help clients reach an informed decision, therapists need to know about alternatives. This can involve being able to engage in discussions concerning the basis on which further therapy is offered, and what else there may be out there that could work equally well or better.

Beneficence

This is about actively doing the greatest good for our clients. During the assessment the definition of what is 'greatest good' can sometimes vary depending on modality and theoretical framework. This will be a question to which we return more in depth when exploring the issue of 'treatments'. Beneficence is about what decision and action will achieve the greatest good (Gabriel and Casemore, 2010, p3). The claim of knowing what is the greatest good rests on insight into other care options. It involves musing over questions such as: What do I mean by 'good'? Good for what? For whom? Why?

Non-maleficence

This guideline involves actively avoiding doing harm. As we shall see, sometimes leaving well alone or referring the client onwards may be the most appropriate options after an assessment. Counselling and psychotherapy involve change, and change usually involves a loss of something familiar, for good or bad. Our decisions during an assessment require careful consideration about the changes that may be involved on an interpersonal, as well as intrapersonal, level for our client. What decisions will cause the least harm?

Justice

As Jenkins (2007, p11) puts it, *the therapist has a duty to promote fairness and equity for all clients*. This means that we need to actively prevent any discrimination on the basis of gender, race, age, disability or sexual orientation and raises questions about our own cultural, social and personal biases. What may 'tint' or blur our lenses when we first look at a case? What do we bring of ourselves to the first consultation? We need also to consider to what extent we can cater for disabled clients, as we could end up discriminating unintentionally by having too high steps or a small toilet, for example.

Self-respect

Saying 'no' can be difficult for many therapists – and not always for altruistic reasons. As referred to earlier, being trustworthy *brings into question the person of the practitioner* (Gabriel and Casemore, 2010, p3). Self-respect is about *fostering the practitioners' self-knowledge and care for self*. As we will see later on, it can form a particularly critical juncture in assessment, with *not taking on more that we can cope with* being an important ground rule. Jenkins reminds us about the different aspects self-care in terms of personal therapy, supervision and ongoing professional training:

> [U]nder the terms of consumer protection law, any professional providing services for money, whether as a plumber or as a psychotherapist, is required to do so with a reasonable care and skill . . . In order to work safely and competently . . . the therapist must work within accepted norms relating to expertise, supervision, work load and continuous development.
> (Jenkins, 2007, p12)

KNOCK, KNOCK . . . WHO'S THERE?

The first meeting can be daunting for both parties. From the therapist's point of view it is a potentially unsafe situation; we are inviting in someone whom we know little more about than that they are experiencing emotional, psychological and practical difficulties. In a study about therapists and safety Despenser found excessive risk-taking by most therapists:

> *In all the settings covered in my survey, the identified risks faced by counsellors are striking: physical isolation, dangerous premises, some*

> *clients being seen without pre-screening, neglect of safety by counsellors and managers. Why do counsellors accept this level of risk?*
>
> (2007, p17)

Despenser alerts us to how personal safety can be a neglected area:

> *Personal safety is an important issue but one that appears to be neglected in counselling literature and in some training. The potential for serious risk posed by clients should not be underestimated.*
>
> (2007, p12)

Malovic-Yeeles connects the therapist's inability to say 'no' and/or to refer onwards to the importance of being strong, helpful and sometimes 'omnipotent'. It is what has often been referred to as the 'rescuing trap' (Hawkins and Shohet, 2006; Bager-Charleson, 2010b). Malovic-Yeeles writes:

> *The hardest part of assessment is to have to say 'no' . . . The most difficult and uncomfortable feeling is recognition and acknowledgement that we, as psychotherapists, are not omnipotent.*
>
> (1998, pp131–2)

Many therapists have indeed experienced both personal crises and subsequent therapy before they set out to become counsellors and psychotherapists themselves. When we approached 280 therapists (Bager-Charleson, 2010b) with the question 'Why did you become a therapist?' the majority referred to a childhood or an adult crisis as a triggering factor (Figure 1.2).

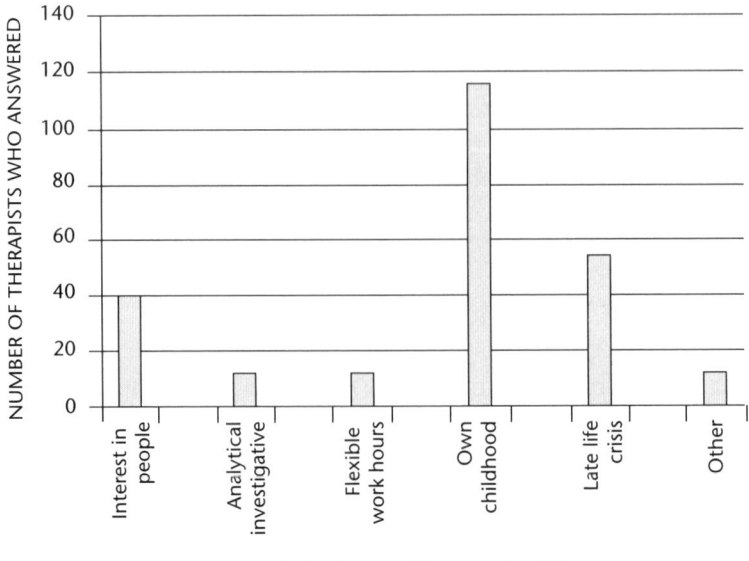

Figure 1.2: Why did you become a therapist? (Bager-Charleson, 2010b)

PERSONAL THERAPY

Personal therapy is regarded by many training institutes as one of the most important learning experiences. Some (Symington, 1986; Jenkins, 2007) contend that psychotherapy must be experienced to be understood. Therapy is, asserts Symington (1986, p9), not a 'thing' that can be taught; it is an experience that occurs between people and *can only be very inadequately communicated to another person*. Jenkins takes a similar stance. He asserts that:

> *[it] requires a process of learning not only about practice, but about ourselves through a therapy which is congruent with our chosen way of practicing the art and science of psychotherapy.*
>
> (2007, px)

Sussman (1992, p4) asserts that our understanding of therapists' underlying motivations is surprisingly meagre: *given the emphasis therapists place on unconscious motivations in human behaviour*, the influence of the therapist's personality and motivations should be questioned more often, and more freely. Sedgwick (1994) and Kottler (1993) suggest that therapists experience shame if they are not personally problem-free. I mentioned earlier how having grown up with a bipolar parent has impacted upon my life. Alice Miller (1997) is critical of the idea of wounded healers; she emphasises the importance of personal therapy to address the 'rescuing trap' of needing our clients to sustain the idea of ourselves as 'omnipotent helpers'. As Guggenbühl-Craig asserts, no person acts from exclusively 'pure' motives: *Even the noblest deeds are based on pure and impure, light and dark, motivations* (2009, p10).

ACTIVITY 1.3

The ethical guideline about self-respect is a valuable reminder of how it is perfectly acceptable for the therapist to respond to their own needs and issues. As suggested earlier, this is an area that is explored in more depth in *Reflective practice in counselling and psychotherapy* (Bager-Charleson, 2010a) and *Why therapists choose to be therapists* (Bager-Charleson 2010b).

Explore the ethical guidelines when approached by a new client for an assessment, with *yourself* in mind. Ask yourself the following questions.

Fidelity
- Am I being true to myself? Do I really want to see this client? Is it right for me, my family and friends, to take on this client at this stage? Do I need more time for myself?

continued overleaf

Autonomy
- Am I considering all factors in my own life when I take on this case? Am I making an informed decision with regard to my own needs and interests? Do I 'know' what I am doing?

Beneficence
- Is this choice serving my own best interests? Am I, for example, considering both short- and long-term effects, for myself psychically and emotionally?

Non-maleficence
- Am I possibly doing myself harm with my decision to take on a new client? Will I have to work evenings or additional hours?

Justice
- What price might I be paying to help others? Am I doing myself justice? Am I being fair to myself? If not, why? And what do I need in order to find a comfortable balance?

Jung (in Sedgwick, 1994, p15) stressed how important it is that *the therapist must at all times keep watch over himself, over the way he is reacting to his patient.* This thinking is illustrated by the psychotherapist Strean who shares his experience as a therapist at an assessment, and subsequent therapy, with his client Mary:

Each time I spoke, trying to persuade her to speak in return, she grew more and more rigid . . . I sighed, gave up, retreated into my silence. Sudden memories of my mother arose. I thought of how much I had wanted her love and how deprived of it I felt when she punished me by refusing to talk to me. Mary represented in many ways the mother I could never satisfy, no matter what I did.
(1998, p13)

Strean's experience highlights both his personal and shared difficulties in meeting others without expectations based on prior experiences. Once he recognises this, Strean acknowledges his failure to meet Mary on her own terms, and after adapting the way he listens, the dynamic in the room changes. Strean reflects:

The analyst should ask, 'Who does this patient remind me of? What emotion or wish or fantasy am I bringing to this analysis that really does not belong but is present because it is a conflictual part of my life?'
(1998, p13)

THE ROLE OF THE ASSESSOR IN PRIVATE PRACTICE

Read the following case study and consider Strean's suggestion that therapists may bring their own wishes and fantasies, which stem from conflicting parts of their lives, to an assessment.

> Case study 1.2
>
> Helen is a 45-year-old counsellor with ten years' experience of both individual and couple work. When Helen was 16 years old, she learned that she was adopted by her grandmother as a baby. Her biological mother was Laura, whom she had considered to be her sister up to this point. Helen's supervisor was reminded of this experience during a session when Helen referred to an assessment of a self-referred couple seeking help at her private practice.
>
> 'I felt sorry for the husband. The wife was the ruthless kind – you know, the real bitchy type who just don't care,' concluded Helen, in what came across to the supervisor as a careless way. Helen spoke louder than usual, used slang and gestures, which reminded the supervisor of a teenager. Helen normally struck the supervisor as a reflective person who chose to consider her own reactions carefully. Her detachment from her new client stood out as unusual, and the supervisor wondered if Helen was communicating something from the session in both words and behaviour.
>
> 'What makes you think that the wife doesn't care?' asked the supervisor.
>
> Helen shrugged her shoulders. 'Don't know,' she said.
>
> 'You don't know . . .?'
>
> 'Well, I suppose it's the whole package. You know, the type with heavy make-up. Giggly, loud, probably just thinking about herself and when to have fun next. Almost tarty . . . well, insincere.'
>
> 'She seems to have stirred some strong feelings in you . . .'
>
> 'I can't stand that type of woman.'
>
> 'Can you describe what feelings you experience in her company?'
>
> Helen shifts restlessly in her chair. She gesticulates, pulls a funny face and laughs a little.
>
> 'I just feel very sorry for him, her husband . . .'
>
> The supervisor remains silent.
>
> 'He must feel so . . .'
>
> Helen shrugs her shoulders again.
>
> 'Well, so boring. So unwanted.'
>
> 'Unwanted?'
>
> 'Well, that's how you feel with that kind of woman . . .'
>
> They both remain silent. Helen's body language changes, she grows still, sighs and adds:
>
> 'She reminds me of my mother, the "sister" who went out dancing all the time . . .'
>
> *continued overleaf*

27

THE ROLE OF THE ASSESSOR IN PRIVATE PRACTICE

> Helen and her supervisor use the rest of the session to unpick the assessment session in a new light after this. Helen recognises that she has assessed the couple through inappropriately tinted lenses.

ACTIVITY 1.4

The case study about Helen focuses on 'lenses' blurred by personal experiences.

- Think of a case where your own personal experiences may have seeped into the assessment. If possible, identify a case where Strean's questions can be addressed, for example: *Who does this patient remind me of? What emotion, wish or fantasy am I bringing to this analysis that really does not belong but is present because it is a conflictual part of my life?*
- The concept of countertransference is usually linked to psychoanalytic theory. How does your training and modality inform you about how to deal with the impact your own emotions may have on your work?

TRANSFERRING OLD EXPERIENCES ON TO NEW ONES

We have reflected upon how the therapist may 'see' clients with blurred vision depending on their own previous experience. This is, of course, also true for clients when they meet their therapist. At our first encounter it is difficult to gauge the 'conscious' and 'unconscious' expectations in the room. The term 'unconscious' is used here in a loose sense, with reference to aspects as yet outside our awareness (Holmes, 1995). It is reasonable to expect that the fantasy of the ultimate parent is one that many people bring with them into therapy, both at the time of assessment and in further therapy. Clients can hope to be cared for and nurtured but also anticipate having to confront dread or real fears. Indeed, Freud based psychotherapy on this assumption and coined the phrase 'transference' with this in mind. In psychoanalytic praxis, one of the main themes is the gradual disentanglement of expected versus real experiences, which are usually brought to the surface by an analysis deliberately aimed at providing space for fantasies to flourish so that they can eventually be questioned by the client themselves.

> **KEY CONCEPTS** Transference
>
> Freud coined the term 'transference' to illustrate how childhood-derived wishes and fantasies could be transferred on to the analyst. Today, transference is used in different contexts. Holmes and Lindley distinguish between:
>
> - *general, 'fleeting' transference where prior hopes, expectations, assumptions and fantasies impinge on interactions with doctors, therapists, and other helpers without being necessarily encouraged or focused upon; and*
> - *'deep' transference, which occurs in therapies which are especially designed to invoke it, for example, through the passivity and reticence of the analyst.*
>
> (1998, p126)
>
> When you read case study 1.3, take on board the following definition of transference:
>
> *Transference refers to the ways in which the feelings, wishes and actions of the patient in relation to the therapist may be unconsciously influenced, coloured and distorted by earlier childhood experiences, especially those with parents.*
>
> Holmes and Lindley (1998, p126)

How people carry expectations based on prior relationships into new ones is something that can be addressed and explored in different ways, depending on the modality. The case study below is intended to illustrate how anticipations based on prior relationships can seep into the therapy even before the parties have met.

> ### Case study 1.3
>
> 'I am sorry,' mumbles Eddie, as he enters the room of Patric, a psychodynamic psychotherapist who runs a private practice from his home in North London.
>   'Eddie? Have a seat,' answers Patric, slightly surprised. 'Why is the middle-aged man in front of him sorry?' he wonders.
>   'This always happens to me,' says Eddie and wipes his forehead with a tissue. 'Sorry, I'm so hot . . . And, well, I might as well come clean . . . I haven't done my homework. There! There you have it . . . and I'm sorry.'
>   'Homework?'
>
> *continued overleaf*

> 'Yes, the homework that you sent me. I put it off, it really bothered me . . . I had nightmares two nights in a row about not being prepared! Last night I dreamt that my boss came to my house. We live in a huge house, and all night I was running around among the kids' toys and our pets, trying to get ready for my boss to arrive at 7pm exactly.' Eddie laughs and puts the tissue in his pocket.
>
> 'To make matters worse, we were going to do a live radio broadcast from the house, and I had this script lying around that I should have practised . . . well, it all went to pot and I woke up in total panic! At first, I thought, "Oh good, it was only a dream", but then I remembered your homework.'
>
> 'You mean the assessment sheet?'
>
> 'Yeah, you've seen me for who I am right from the start . . . a cheat and a liar – well, not a liar, perhaps, but a failure. I couldn't arrange a piss-up in a brewery – always letting folks down. I'm sorry . . .'

COMMENT

Patric is taken back by Eddie's outburst. He has established a habit of sending out an assessment sheet with some questions, which he encourages his clients to 'look through' before their first meeting. He realises that he and Eddie have interpreted the intentions regarding the form differently and that the form has stirred a reaction in Eddie that he has not seen, as yet, in any of his other clients. Eddie also discloses that he has chosen Patric from among other therapists on the basis of his degree in biology, which again surprises Patric, as he has forgotten that this detail is mentioned on his website. Towards the end of their first interview, Patric knows more about Eddie's background. He knows that Eddie is fifty years old, married, has two children and works from home on his web design business as a result of 'not enjoying the politics that goes with working in an organisation'. As Eddie leaves, Patric has a distinct sensation of being perceived as an intolerant, strict father, the professor in biology whom Eddie has referred to with dread during the session. As Eddie leaves the house after further therapy has been agreed upon, his last words are: 'I hope I won't let you down.'

ACTIVITY 1.5

- Transference is a concept used in psychoanalysis and psychodynamic theory. Consider how your training and modality informs you to deal with situations like these, perhaps ultimately revolving around people's difficulties in being 'real' or 'authentic' enough to engage in meetings in the 'here and now' without 'baggage' and undue expectations.

PROMISES AND CONTRACTS

Compared to therapists in the NHS or other organisational settings, private practitioners have to actively market their services. Withers (2007), Jenkins (2007) and Mitchels and Bond (2010) highlight the importance of careful consideration when advertising counselling and psychotherapy services through *Yellow Pages*, newspapers or the internet. Being realistic about what we offer is paramount for both the client's welfare and the therapist's. Private practitioners are vulnerable to accusations of misrepresentation, and Withers reminds us of the importance of considering what fantasies the client may begin to nurture before therapy begins. The client will perhaps have been 'shopping around' – specialisation, location and fees are some of the obvious considerations. However, in private practice the client can also consider their choice of therapist with reference to gender, social, ethnic or educational background, and other characteristics that carry different meanings to different people. The notion of choice can feed into unrealistic expectations. Withers writes:

> *For the client, the notion of choice brings with it far greater scope to demand practical arrangements, negotiate terms, request a particular mode of therapy or a particular kind of therapist. While some of this may be reasonable, and brings a reminder of adult-to-adult relating into what can become an infantilising and disempowering process for the client, it has the disadvantage of feeding a fantasy that the ultimate parent, endlessly attuned to one's needs, can be found and purchased.*
>
> (2007, p52)

It is tempting to want to 'stand out' and attract attention when advertising. Yet the ability to remain within one's professional remit lies at the heart of our duty of care. Mitchels and Bond warn us to *beware of making extravagant promises and predicting outcomes*. They continue:

> *Therapists should be realistic and pragmatic, remembering that responsibility for the outcome of therapy depends largely on the client . . . So, to avoid claims of misrepresentation or breach of contract, it is most unwise to make extravagant claims for therapy and, as Cohen says, 'the wisest of them promise nothing at all'.*
>
> (2010, p43)

The more transparent the therapeutic goals are, the less likely we are to be targets for complaints regarding unrealistic expectations. A very structured assessment form at the beginning of the therapy can sometimes be used to protect the therapist rather than benefiting the client. Mitchels and Bond write:

> *Some complaints may arise from clients who feel that they have not been 'cured' as they had hoped. They may have had unrealistic expectations . . . of themselves, and/or the therapist may not have had the necessary skill to address the client's issues appropriately . . . Assessment can identify the need, hopes and expectations of the client. Following on from this, the discussion, negotiation and agreement of the therapeutic contract is vitally important.*
>
> (2010, pp42–3)

It is essential to allow time to discuss expectations and to seek some kind of consent, if only to agree not to be specific. Consent does not have to involve fixed targets and objectives; the main aim is to ensure that both parties agree to the same thing. Jenkins writes:

> *Consent, to be effective, must stem from a knowledgeable decision based on adequate information about the therapy, the available alternatives and the collateral risks.*
>
> (Mitchels and Bond, 2010, p50)

Some therapists choose to put their agreements in writing although there are currently no regulations for private practitioners governing written contracts. Mitchels and Bond write:

> *[I]n some circumstances oral contracts might not present any difficulties. However, if the contract is not written down, the lack of any evidence of what has been agreed might become problematic . . . [I]n the event of a dispute there is often no way of satisfactorily establishing what occurred.*
>
> (2010, p50)

KEY CONCEPTS   Contractual themes

Contracts usually involve two themes. Dale (2008, p1) refers to these two areas in terms of the following.

1. The 'business side' of the agreement.
    - ✓ When and how often will you meet?
    - ✓ Are sessions open-ended or for a limited time?
    - ✓ What are the fees?
    - ✓ What happens in the case of cancellations or unattended sessions?
    - ✓ If you ask for details of the client's GP, be clear about what might impel you to contact the GP. Explain the limits of your confidentiality. Dale writes:

> *Confidentiality is rarely, if ever, absolute . . . Most counsellors would want to break confidentiality in the case of harm to self or others . . . and this needs to be made clear to the client.*
>
> (2008, p2)
>
> 2. The 'process side' of the contract. This aspect concerns:
>   ✓ mutual understanding of the client's reasons for coming to therapy; and
>   ✓ what the client can expect to happen next.

As already suggested, it is of key importance that in consent in general and in contracts specifically both parties agree to the same thing. Agreeing on what will happen next might, for some therapists, involve specific targets such as *return to work, talk to three friends, cook two meals* (Dale, 2008, p3). Other therapists may prefer 'process contracts', which are ultimately based on *what the client wants to talk about and their ultimate goals*. Some therapists prefer fluid contracts that will be revisited and developed as the work proceeds. Indeed, as Aveline contends:

> *How clients see the problem initially will nearly always be different from later on in therapy. Their view of the terrain will be enlarged and hidden aspects may become visible . . . the counsellor [needs] to be vigilant and to reassess frequently where the intervention is going and could go.*
>
> (1997, p112)

Fluid contracts are in this sense not only tolerated but sometimes preferred. Dale stresses that each therapist will need to adjust their contract to their own modality. Whether the contract becomes specific or fluid, the important thing is that a tentative consent is reached about what to expect before the therapy begins.

SHOULD WE USE QUESTIONNAIRES IN ASSESSMENT?

As we shall explore later on, questionnaires are a valuable means of gathering information on many levels, ranging from the content of the actual replies to how the client feels about answering these kinds of questions in the first place. They also provide the therapist with both transparency surrounding the proceedings and the client's consent in case misunderstandings around expectations arise further on in the treatment. There are no straight answers to whether or not one should use assessment questionnaires.

Milner and O'Byrne (2004) assert that *many experienced counsellors simply have a list of criteria in their head* when assessing their clients for the first time. They conclude that:

> *Most counsellors never use questionnaires . . . Many counsellors believe that clients find them intimidating and off-putting, or at least prefer to use them with a client after they have established some rapport and trust.*
> (2004, p46)

Daines et al. (2007, p28), on the other hand, strongly advise the use of questionnaires. They consider it 'unwise' – unethical even – when assessments *allow issues to emerge over a period of time from the material that the client chooses to disclose rather than asking questions or undertaking a formal process of assessment.*

There is not yet much research with reported benefits of pre-assessment questionnaires in private practice, but there are studies within organisations such as the National Health Service (NHS), and these are explored further in Biljana's chapters. Mace found that asking clients to complete questionnaires prior to assessment interviews helped to:

- *gather factual information, with advantages such as comprehension, prior reflection and greater freedom during the interview;*
- *prepare the client for the interview and for what psychotherapy entails;*
- *reduce non-attendance;*
- *assess the client's 'readiness', in terms of attitude towards and motivation for psychotherapy;*
- *demonstrate the client's perception and outlook;*
- *enable the assessor to focus the interview;*
- *provide data for research;*
- *allow diagnosis and prioritisation;*
- *save the assessor's time;*
- *facilitate the choice of assessor for the subsequent interview.*

(1995a, p207)

Holmes agrees with the value of 'form-filling', but does not want it to interfere with the initial contact:

> *Form-filling is necessary, especially in these days of audit, managerial control and research, but I prefer to ask the patient to do it after we have met rather than before.*
> (1995, p29)

A COMMON LANGUAGE?

Questionnaires with commonly held categorisations of symptoms and set goals may become a necessary part of independent practice, as part of the general tendency towards the professionalisation of counselling and psychotherapy.

Barkham et al. (2010) draw our attention to how questionnaires have developed over time. There is an ongoing attempt to combine standardised information with the client's own narratives, and Barkham et al. (2010) cite the development of the Clinical Outcomes in Routine Evaluation – Outcome Measure (CORE-OM) as an example of this. They assert that CORE-OM is a valid, reliable and accessible measure for clients and practitioners in multiple settings and in different ways. CORE-OM is an example of a questionnaire that can be used as a collaborative experience; standardised questions can be addressed by therapists and clients together. The scores can become stepping stones for further enquiry into the client's unique set of experiences (Van Rijn, 2010, p118).

> ### REFLECTION POINT
>
> How do questionnaires fit in with your practice and theoretical framework? If you feel unsure, consider the issue in the light of the ethical guidelines referred to earlier. Do questionnaires help with:
>
> - fidelity and doing what you said you would do?
> - autonomy and allowing clients to make informed choices?
> - beneficence and duty to care?
> - non-maleficence and 'never do any harm'?
> - justice and treating clients fairly?
> - self-respect?

ASSESSING 'READINESS' FOR THERAPY

During the first interview it is important to consider to what extent the client appears to be equipped to address and challenge the way they are leading their lives. In the case of Eddie (see case study 1.3), for example, it will be important for Patric to consider whether or not Eddie is in a place where he can challenge his perceptions of himself and the world around him. It will be essential for Patric to monitor and treat Eddie's defences with utmost respect.

THE ROLE OF THE ASSESSOR IN PRIVATE PRACTICE

> **Case study 1.4**
>
> After his first encounter with Eddie, Patric makes a note to tread carefully. He wants to assess Eddie's ego strength a bit more. There may be a perfectly natural explanation for Eddie's flustered appearance; he may always get nervous or overexcited in new situations and may feel perfectly comfortable with that. The behaviour may, on the other hand, be a sign of an unhelpful, dysfunctional pattern of engaging with the world around him – perhaps, ponders Patric, on the basis of an internalised image of himself as an unlovable, useless, unworthy little boy. If so, Patric will need to know more about the origins of Eddie's expectations regarding relationships and self-image. If Eddie hasn't addressed these issues before, Patric will need <u>to assess Eddie's capacity to cope with a potentially new way of looking at himself and the world around him</u>. To what extent will Eddie's family life allow him to potentially re-evaluate his relationships and his general outlook on life? Is there space for fundamental changes in these areas? What would be the outcome if Eddie explored his identity in a new light?
>
> On the other hand, it may not be like this at all. Patric may be making too much out of Eddie's anxiety around the questionnaire and the link between their 7pm appointment and Eddie's dream.
>
> Patric makes a double-loop assessment of his interpretation of Eddie and feels obliged to make a note of his own envy with regard to Eddie's 'huge house' as Patric lives in a small flat. He decides to talk to his supervisor about being too ready to pathologise Eddie as a result of needing to hold on to a sense of power.
>
> Patric also decides to pay close attention to Eddie's own narratives. He is interested in Eddie's 'stories' about himself and others.

COMMENT

Patric is left with a rich tapestry of information about Eddie. An important fact, as Patric concludes, is to take into account how therapy frequently disrupts the status quo. Ways of behaving and relating to people have often developed for a reason; what has become dysfunctional and, perhaps, counterproductive in present and ongoing relationships may have served an important need to protect the self at another stage in life. Aveline (1997) reminds us never to dispel coping skills without being confident that new ones are in place or realistic to obtain. Aveline writes:

> *The assessor has responsibility for gauging potential gains and losses through therapy and discussing these with the client so that he or she can make an informed choice about processing . . . A person's defences, however inappropriate and out of date they are now, were needed ways of coping*

with difficult situations in the past and should not be forced to yield except as new strengths develop.

(1997, p111)

This stance calls for a careful consideration of *potential gains and losses*, as Aveline puts it. Sometimes 'leaving well alone' can be the most appropriate option. Aveline writes:

[Sometimes] leaving well alone may be the right course when the therapist judges that the client's inner world is so fragile that . . . the client has insufficient personal resources to make any developmental moves.

(1997, p109)

In the case study with Eddie, the term 'ego strength' was used. In a broad sense the concept highlights degrees of emotional stability and the ability to tolerate different, and sometimes conflicting, perspectives of oneself and relationships. This often involves being *willing to consider conflicts on an interpersonal level* as well as intrapsychic constraints (Strupp and Binder, 1984). There is, indeed, often *an artificial distinction drawn between the inner psychological worlds of thought, emotion and conflict and the external world of action* (Aveline, 1997, p106). Perhaps not surprisingly, what happens in the outside world affects our inner worlds and vice versa; and it is often this interrelation upon which therapy is centred. A subject that Biljana will return to in the following chapters is how important it can be to address the issue of change when assessing a client's readiness for therapy. Roffey-Barentsen and Malthouse stress how change often involves a degree of loss: *Change means loss . . . you will have lost an element that made up a part of what you were* (2009, p20).

Some therapists may choose to assess a client's 'readiness' tentatively as in Eddie's case. To conceptualise how difficult change can be, different models can facilitate a discussion about the cost involved in making such changes. As illustrated by Biljana's references in later chapters, there are different ways to approach change. The ABC model in Table 1.1 explains how client and therapist can jointly examine the often very 'good' and usually unexplored reasons for dodging changes.

Case study 1.5

This is an example from couple therapy where Emma and Alan explore their lack of closeness. Alan, in particular, examines his excessive working habits and lack of involvement in his family life. Alan is the instigator of the therapy and says that he wants to 'save the relationship before it is too late'. Emma is tired of him

continued overleaf

working long days and most weekends. She says that she is beginning to lose patience. Alan strikes the therapist as very motivated and committed to the relationship, but as they begin to explore both the positive and negative aspects of a closer relationship, underlying fears become tangible.

Alan's mother committed suicide when Alan was five years old. He recalls how he and his mother were 'very close'; Alan was his mother's 'little helper'.

'Some helper!' mocked Alan in a self-punishing way.

The therapist uses a flip chart and explores each theme with her client. The outcome of the ABC exploration of what change may be involved for Alan, is presented in Table 1.1.

The ABC model (Tschudi, cited in Tindall, 1994) helps them to explore forces that may prevent Alan from making the changes he appears so committed to make. The ABC model (Table 1.1) reveals an underlying tension between core constructs, which he holds on to with safety in mind. It helps them to gauge that beneath the surface of the seemingly straightforward premise of 'I want to spend more time with my family' there lingers a construct that being close equals loss (C1, in Table 1.1). Distance can, perhaps, protect from this loss. Furthermore, the ABC model can help to assess the 'cost' involved in change, by highlighting underlying tensions between core constructs.

COMMENT

The ABC model illustrates an attempt to explore the presented problem from different angles. It can be used as a tool to conceptualise why certain changes can be so hard to put into action. It can also open up a discussion about themes and patterns and, in a sense, 'diagnose' common denominators among problems and symptoms associated with the 'presented problem'. It is usually important to address the fact that therapy does not require change as such; sensitively and collaboratively conducted therapy involves throwing light on sometimes obscured options and alternatives. Therapy is perhaps ultimately concerned with exploring choices and is not about right or wrong ways of leading our lives. The ABC chart offered Alan the opportunity to consider whether or not his defence would serve his purposes in the future. It presents clients with an insight into what possible areas therapy may delve into and opens up at an early stage a discussion about potential themes and topics to be addressed.

In couple therapy, the therapist usually makes a point of exploring both partners' underlying values and beliefs about their presented and preferred options, with a view to forming a working hypothesis about, for example, marital 'fit'. Psychodynamic therapists work with a particular focus on 'unconscious' factors that have brought the couple together: did they share

A1 Present position	A2 Preferred position
• I always work, I can't find time for my wife and our boy.	• I would like to spend more time with my family.
B1 Disadvantages of present position	**B2 Advantages of preferred position**
• I become obsessed by work and end up exhausted, detached and lonely. • I turn inwardly for help, I struggle with delegating tasks and lose out on valuable connection and closeness, no sense of belonging.	• I will belong and feel more part of my family. • I will delegate at work, and let others take responsibility. • I will feel healthier, less exhausted and overworked.
C1 Advantages of present position	**C2 Disadvantages of preferred position**
• Independence at work and absences for home protect me; only turning to myself puts me in control of events. • I rely on no one but myself; I am in control of my own life and I cannot be disappointed when others let me down or I lose them. And I will not let others down . . . (or 'kill them off').	• Not working all the time, and enjoying my family makes me dependent on them for my happiness. • Opening up for others means being open for pain, and loss. • It hurts too much to be abandoned and let down again, I couldn't face that again. Closeness would leave me open to that risk.

Table 1.1: The ABC model

Source: originally based on Tschudi, cited in Tindall, 1994.

the same type of defence, or did they perhaps complement each other? It appears as if Alan has always adopted a distance to intimate relationships. Why would Emma make a point of choosing a partner who withdraws? Did that have anything to do with the fact that Emma's father was, according to her own account, overpowering and domineering? If so, have their respective 'defences' – originally developed to protect themselves from loss (Alan) and being dominated and overpowered (Emma) – now turned against them, preventing them from having their needs met? Old defences can become restricting cages in later life. Could this be the case in Alan's and Emma's lives?

The therapist may also explore the relationship with a systemic perspective. In what way do Alan and Emma's respective behaviours sustain and maintain their problems? Perhaps, for instance, Emma becomes more 'nagging' when Alan 'withdraws', which causes him to withdraw further, and so on?

In both ways of approaching the ABC model the client's own input is explored. As suggested, this can result not only in the loss of familiar ways of relating to and perceiving the world, but also in changes to actual circumstances in family life, work etc. Some therapists prefer working in the opposite order, and begin with behaviours in the here and now, with underlying 'defence' systems tapped into eventually, if needed.

RISK ASSESSMENT

The idea of a 'price tag' to change suggests a contribution from the client, sometimes a sacrifice. Ruddell and Curwen reflect upon how the ability to explore one's own contribution to the problem is a significant sign of 'readiness' for therapy:

> *A client who seeks counselling is likely to have already acknowledged that they have a problem or that they would like to change some aspects of their life . . . Readiness for counselling also requires that individuals recognise, if only in a small way, that they contribute to their difficulties.*
>
> (1997, p73)

To explore the 'cost' of change usually requires being able to 'loop back' both emotionally and cognitively on one's own values, beliefs and behaviour reflexively. In a tentative discussion during the assessment phase, the therapist will often need to consider whether the client seems likely to cope with new and other ways of framing situations. The degree of this ability may impact on the therapeutic relationship. As Cooper and Alfillé put it, can the client *explore the reasons why he is where he is in life*? They write:

> *[When assessing the potential suitability of a client] we must try to assess ego strength . . . and look at the defences that the patient uses. It has to be remembered that defences must be respected . . . they may be preventing complete disintegration, being used to protect an extremely fragile ego. We need to gauge the patient's ability to tolerate feelings of guilt . . . Can he move back and forth in historical time and make connections while relating his history? Above all, is he curious to explore the reasons why he is where he is in life?*
>
> (1998, p136)

In a similar vein, in their selection criteria for the assessor to consider during the first interview, Strupp and Binder include the abilities to reflect and engage with curiosity in the therapeutic process (1984, cited in Aveline 1997, p110). They contend that the client 'should':

- be sufficiently discomforted by their feelings or behaviour to seek help in the first place;
- have sufficient basic trust to attend regularly and talk about their life;
- be willing to consider conflicts on an interpersonal level;
- be prepared to examine feelings;
- have sufficient capacity for mature relationships where conflicts can be collaboratively examined.

Kächele and Thomä put this in a different way:

Sick enough to need it, and healthy enough to stand it.
(cited in Malovic-Yeeles, 1998, p128)

Cooper and Alfillé (1998, p136) stress that *the difference between assessing for therapy in an institution or clinic, as opposed to private practice, must be . . . borne in mind*. With safety issues and referral options in mind, it can be argued that it is particularly important to consider contraindications for potential suitability in private practice. Clarksson uses the metaphor of 'plumbing' to illustrate how the assessment involves careful consideration of how 'accessible' the client may be:

[The initial meeting is at its simplest level] equivalent to agreeing with a plumber at what time to arrive where, to do what and for how much money. And of course, in order for the plumber to do his or her work, the householder needs to agree to have the water supply turned off for the period that the plumber may be working with the pipes.
(1995, p33)

ACTIVITY 1.6

When assessing the 'readiness' and suitability for therapy, Ruddell and Curwen (1997, p79) suggest that therapists consider to what extent the potential client:

- acknowledges problems;
- recognises their own contribution to the difficulties;
- demonstrates motivation.

Aveline stresses the importance of being *realistic about one's own ability as a counsellor* (1997, p113).

- Can you think of an example where you would consider it sensible not to offer further treatment of a client?

CHAPTER SUMMARY

Assessment in private practice involves a greater freedom of choice than in organisations and agencies. On the other hand, the therapist is often alone if anything goes wrong and needs to invest in support, advice and critical feedback. In this chapter we have explored strategies to assess our own impact on a client's problems.

- We have looked at the important role of the BACP ethical framework (BACP, 2010) in private practice, where priorities and choices are less determined by an organisation ethos and overall policy.
- Ongoing supervision, peer support and personal therapy are referred to as essential means of securing feedback and support for the therapist. We have looked at personal therapy and supervision as methods of feedback for the therapist on an emotional, ethical and professional level.
- We have considered the difference between one-person and two-person psychologies. The latter emphasises the relationship and the mutual impact the therapist and the client have on each other and on the overall work. The assessor is no longer a 'sterile surgeon' who can leave his personal and cultural values and beliefs completely outside the room. We have considered the idea of a 'double-loop' assessment to address the therapist's own underlying personal, theoretical and cultural assumptions which may be brought into the assessment and ongoing therapy.
- We have explored the meaning of 'doing no harm' in the context of contracts, self-awareness and ways of relating to clients. The therapist will need to recognise his or her own limits and, as Aveline puts it, approach the client while taking the following into consideration: *Do I have sufficient time, interest and relevant skills for the therapy of this client. If not, who has?* (1997, p113).

SUGGESTED FURTHER READING

Bager-Charleson, S (2010) *Reflective practice in counselling and psychotherapy.* Exeter: Learning Matters.

The book examines therapeutic practice in a context of cultural forces, different modalities and the therapist's own personal input. It includes theory and experiential exercises to assist students, trainees and new graduates in their case study and essay writing, supervision and general discussions around reflective therapeutic practice.

Claringbull, N (2011) *Mental health in counselling and psychotherapy.* Exeter: Learning Matters.

This book explores mental health issues that you are likely to come across in practice. It looks at problems such as anxiety, depression, stress, addiction, phobias and certain behavioural problems that are sometimes diagnosed as 'disorders'. Issues surrounding the mental health spectrum are explained in the context of recent mental health legislation and referrals, and the ways in which therapists can best help their clients are explored.

Green, J (2010) *Creating the therapeutic relationship in counselling and psychotherapy.* Exeter: Learning Matters.

This is a helpful guide for those with an interest in how to engage with clients in a therapeutic process based on trust. This book explores the personal qualities and attitudes of the therapist and considers ways of being fully present and emotionally available in their encounters with clients.

BACP information sheets

The British Association for Counsellors and Psychotherapists provides all its members with free information sheets in all areas of practice.

Visit **www.bacp.co.uk/information/information_sheets.php** for further details.

These information sheets cover many fields, from ethical, legal and theoretical issues to more hands-on matters such as contract making and marketing. They are an invaluable resource when dealing with ambiguous matters such as how to deal with signs of child sexual abuse, suicide risks or signs of serious mental health issues.

CHAPTER 2

'Diagnosing' problems

> **CORE KNOWLEDGE**
> - This chapter focuses on the issue of 'formulating a hypothesis' about further treatment. It looks at what a hypothesis is and at the clinical, ethical and moral guidelines for formulating one.
> - We will consider the differences and overlapping features between diagnosis, formulation and assessment.
> - The issue of realistic expectations is carried through into this chapter, and both safety and referrals will be explored in depth.

INTRODUCTION

As suggested earlier, the BACP ethical guidelines strongly advise that the therapist should *be realistic and pragmatic* and avoid making *extravagant claims for therapy* (Mitchels and Bond 2010, p43). 'Diagnosis' can have medical connotations and it is important to consider the concept with an open mind. Many prefer to use the term 'formulation', which often emphasises the importance of regarding any hypothesis as part of an ongoing, collaborative strategy. Johnstone and Dallos quote Roy-Chowdhury who writes:

> *Therapy/formulation [aims] to seek to understand and make sense of another's experience and to offer these provisional and tentative understandings to the other for consideration.*
>
> (2006, p113)

Johnstone and Dallos contend that a clinical formulation should ideally draw on an *ongoing collaborative sense-making* (2006, p231). The therapist should *offer formulations tentatively and be constantly aware of the need to reformulate*. Bateman and Holmes (2002, p140) suggest that we consider *two strands of the assessment* and highlight a *dual function of the assessor*. Our first interview involves being *engaging enough for a meaningful encounter with the patient to happen, while at the same time remaining sufficiently objective.* Bateman and Holmes contend that the role of the assessor is both to *sit beside* and *to sum up strengths and weaknesses*:

> *The word 'assessment' is derived from the Latin assidere, to sit beside, but also contains overtones of legal assizes, and the assessment of taxes, in which an individual's assets are reckoned and weighed in the balance. There are thus two strands in the assessment interview: an empathic attempt by the analyst to grasp the nature of the patient's predicament, and a more distanced effort to sum up his strengths and weaknesses.*
>
> (2002, p140)

The concept of 'diagnosis' carries medical connotations that fall outside the domains of counselling and psychotherapy. There are, however, some principles of diagnosis that can be helpful to transfer into therapy. Ultimately, diagnosis is all about *finding commonalities*. Ruddell writes:

> *Diagnosis is concerned with classifying a problem . . . Diagnosis begins with a consideration of signs and symptoms. Signs are externally observable: sneezing, giggling, inability to make eye contact . . . Symptoms are [also] subjective: headache, hearing voices not heard by others, or feeling 'low'. In medical diagnosis, it is common to detect the cause of the signs and symptoms (aetiology) as well as consider their development (pathogenesis). In psychiatric diagnosis aetiology is more usually inferred . . . there is not a known cause . . . while certain chemicals or hormones might be in evidence in the body of a person with heightened anxiety, these cannot be said to have caused the anxiety.*
>
> (2009, p8)

Ruddell highlights here how diagnosis in the case of the mind invariably rests on a different cause-and-effect line of 'evidence' to that of medical evidence. A psychiatric diagnosis involves grouping symptoms and signs together in clusters termed 'syndromes' or 'disorders', which change over time and which ultimately are subject to interpretation. Symptoms indicating a case of measles and mumps are different from symptoms of, for instance, depression. Since 1992 the American Psychiatric Association (APA) has made a number of attempts to gather and categorise all the recognized mental health disorders in one coherent handbook. The DSM-IV-TR, the *Diagnostic and statistical manual of mental disorders*, 4th edition (2000) is the most recent version, which bridges between the earlier DSM-IV and DSM-V to reflect latest research findings. Red spots and swollen tonsils are a different type of evidence to the descriptive categorisations offered in DSM-IV, with depression 'diagnosed' on the basis of gloominess and pessimism as well as feelings of worthlessness, self/blaming and guilt (American Psychiatric Association, 2000). If we diagnosed people from these categories alone, most people would be diagnosed as depressed. As Ruddell stresses,

- fidelity and doing what you say you will do;
- autonomy and allowing clients to make informed choices;
- beneficence and duty of care;
- non-maleficence and 'never do any harm to anyone';
- justice and treating clients fairly;
- self-respect and looking after yourself.

WHAT ARE WE LOOKING FOR – AND WHY?

As suggested at the beginning of this section, the ethical principles of beneficence and non-maleficence involve a commitment to achieving the 'greatest good' for our clients and to doing them the 'least harm'. How do we know that we do good? On what basis do we judge what is the 'greatest good'? Hinshelwood stresses that the 'truth' of our hypothesis lies in to what extent it resonates with the client:

> [T]he nature of psychotherapy is the intuitive production of hypotheses – they are for trying out with the patient. We do not work to build up evidence before making hypotheses as in other forms of science; in fact the reverse, the process of therapy is to try out hypotheses with the patient. Our evidence comes from watching their fate. The response to an interpretation is then the criterion for deciding whether to retain the hypothesis or abandon it.
>
> (1995, p156)

In this sense diagnosing and forming hypotheses in therapy follow some different ground rules to other forms of science. There will always be the matter of interpretation at the heart of things, and this makes it all the more important to be sensitive towards the reaction of the client.

HOW DO WE KNOW THAT THERAPY HELPS?

The answer to this question depends on what we mean by 'knowing'. Cardinal et al. remind us that knowledge is ultimately a word, and that all our words are used in a context and can therefore mean different things:

> Philosophers have put a lot of energy into the search for a definition [of knowledge] but none has been entirely successful . . . Perhaps knowledge is similar to concepts like 'bald' or 'heap', which have no precise definition but have hazy boundaries.
>
> (2004, p141)

In today's debate about evidence-based practice, the term 'evidence' is sometimes confused with hardcore facts and impermeable truths. Barkham et al. reflect upon evidence as follows:

> *What is evidence? Simply put, it is the basis for a belief. Beliefs may arise from a number of sources. Two major sources of relevance to health services are personal experience and scientific research.*
>
> (2010, p5)

Outcome research is an area to which we will return in the following chapters on organisations, where time and money push the issue of usefulness to the forefront. However, regardless of setting, professionals are likely to want to do a 'good' job and would probably all welcome evidence of doing their job right.

The CORE questionnaire referred to above illustrates the increased emphasis paid to 'evidence' within therapy and other helping professions. Standardised questionnaires do not guarantee quality as such, but they can certainly help us to pinpoint and focus on certain parts of our practice. An important issue raised by the emphasis on evidence-based practice is the benefits of being able to communicate about what we do, or at least what we think or hope that we do. The terms evidence-based treatment (EBT) and empirically supported treatment (EST) refer to interventions that are accessible enough to be systematically tested and evaluated by outsiders. It puts the knowledge that we have in context where, ideally, everyone relates to certain core symptoms with the same meanings in mind. Exploring client symptoms and different forms of interventions in terms of 'core' symptoms provides practitioners with a platform where certain shared aspects of the work can be addressed, sometimes challenged, and ideally developed and improved. Davies et al. write:

> *The unifying theme in all definitions is that evidence (however construed) can be independently observed and verified, and that there is a broad consensus as to its contents (if not its interpretation).*
>
> (2000, p3)

A valuable outcome of evidence-based thinking may also be the level of transparency between therapists and their clients that the option of addressing 'core' issues allows. As suggested earlier, all human beings are likely to interpret almost all new situations from different angles and with a different focus. And many therapists argue that it is their job to step into their client's shoes as much as possible and see situations from their perspective when 'sieving' for information. This is important to remember in whatever way we encounter a new client. Take some time to consider the next case study and consider in what way the therapist, Liza, 'sieves' and reaches her formulation of the 'problem'.

Case study 2.2

Liza describes her work as person-centred. She runs her private practice from home and has a diploma in person-centred counselling. She has also worked for a church-run pro-life agency. She finds that her pro-life experience has helped her to develop skills in addition to her formal counselling training.

The woman in front of her is called Paula. She is in her thirties, newly divorced and with three children. Paula feels 'listless', and her GP has suggested counselling for what he described as 'getting back on her feet' after the divorce. During her assessment session with Liza, Paula recounts her life. She tells her about divorced parents, teenage problems with bulimia and several failed relationships, one of them resulting in a pregnancy and subsequent abortion. This is an extract from their first interview:

Paula sits down in a seemingly relaxed way.

'You know . . . I'd say that I have been depressed off and on for as long as I can remember.'

Liza has been waiting for a cue to bring up a subject that she feels has been left hanging in the air. She says: 'You mentioned an abortion in your teens . . .'

'Yes . . .?'

'Would you perhaps want to talk more about that . . .?'

Silence.

Paula shrugs her shoulders.

The clinical experience at the pro-life agency has helped Liza to develop a theory about abortion as a means of self-harm; she feels aware of what a terrible burden women who have terminated a pregnancy live with; the guilt of having killed their own baby is something that her supervisor at the previous agency explored as 'killing of a bit of themselves'. With this in mind, Liza feels able to throw new light on Paula's ongoing depression. Paula is still quiet, but Liza is not surprised; it is a difficult subject to talk about and she wants to help Paula on her way.

'What made you decide in the end to go for an abortion?'

'There wasn't really anything in particular . . . I was just a child myself at the time.'

Liza nods.

'It's not easy . . .'

'No, decisions like that are never easy.'

'No . . . and so the baby was really you, wasn't it . . .?

'Pardon?'

'The baby was that tiny, vulnerable, needy part of you that you had to get rid of.' Liza is aware that their therapy has not yet started, but she wants to show Paula that this is a safe place to connect with deep, sometimes hidden, strong emotions.

> Paula frowns.
> 'I suppose what I'm saying is that to bring someone into the world like that, well . . . I couldn't look after it properly and I had to take responsibility as best as I could.'
> Silence.
> 'I can't really see that has something to do with my depression . . .'
> 'You seem to have been caught between wanting to look after someone in the way you weren't looked after and wanting somebody to love you . . .' replies Liza.
> Silence. Liza eventually continues.
> 'I mean, perhaps like killing a part of yourself . . .'
> Silence.
> The day after, Paula leaves a message on Liza's answering machine. She says that she is not interested in further therapy.

COMMENT

Liza's own agenda manifested itself, as some of her own underpinning values seeped into the room without her awareness. A major problem with Liza's approach lies with the difference between what Argyris and Schön (1978) would call her 'espoused' theory and her 'theory-in-use'. Simply speaking, a gap like this means that we do not always practise what we preach. Argyris and Schön found that people often considered themselves as adhering to a certain way of working but that they actually went and did something quite different. Many would have an 'espoused theory' to which they officially had committed themselves, which, as in Liza's case, could differ from what they actually put into practice. Argyris and Schön write:

> *When someone is asked how he would behave under certain circumstances, the answer he usually gives is his espoused theory of action for that situation. This is the theory of action to which he gives allegiance, and which, upon request, he communicates to others. However, the theory that actually governs his actions is this theory-in-use.*
>
> (1978, pp6–7)

In Liza's case, her person-centred theory puts an emphasis on the internalisation of the individual's 'locus of evaluation'. Her espoused theory rests on the importance of enabling people to rediscover their own values, beliefs and life purpose. Being taught to mistrust one's own judgements is something that can lead to a lack of an internal locus of evaluation. The role of therapy is to facilitate an environment that strengthens the individual's capacity to trust their own thoughts and feelings when making decisions or choosing courses of action, rather than always turning to

'DIAGNOSING' PROBLEMS

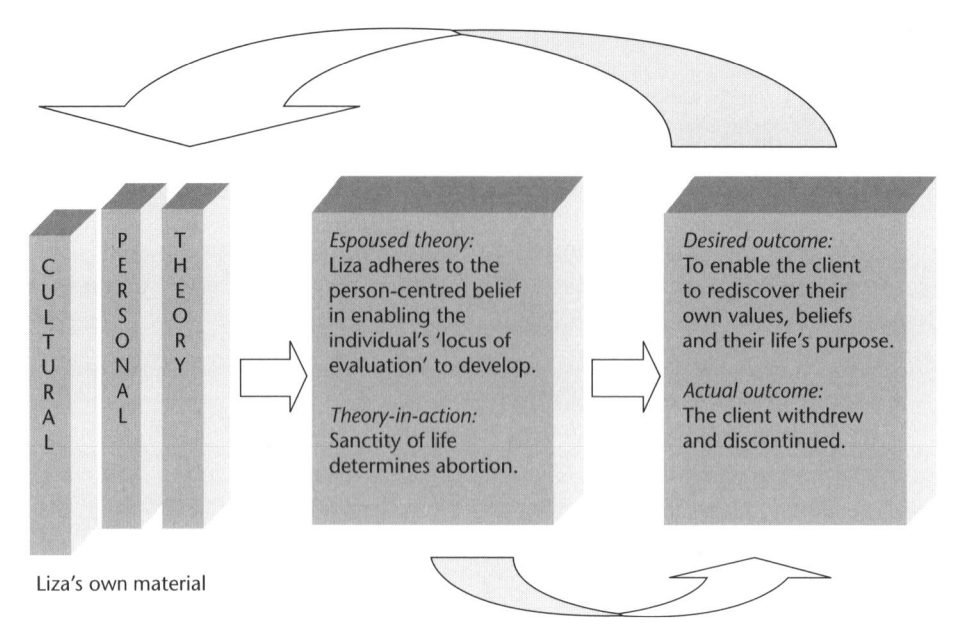

Figure 2.1: Liza's double-loop thinking on strategy and outcome, focusing on her espoused theory versus her theory-in-action

external authorities or being paralysed by indecision. Liza's supervisor triggered a double-loop assessment of the problem (see Figure 2.1) in which Liza herself became part of the problem, showing that her underlying assumptions about abortion affected the outcome of the interview.

Supervision highlights the value of 'critical friends' who can be trusted to contribute with new and 'foreign' angles, and this is illustrated in Case study 2.3.

Case study 2.3

Paula chose to discontinue her therapy with Liza, who was not completely surprised; it had happened before. She is aware from her time at the pro-life agency that people sometimes struggle to talk about abortion – it is a taboo area. Single-loop learning can be compared to the action of a thermostat that switches off and on at a certain temperature. Translated into therapy, single-loop learning concerns conclusions reached 'automatically'; Liza does not question her own input to the problem. She considers Paula to be in denial, maybe not ready to talk yet . . .

When Liza brings up her case in supervision, the supervisor challenges her focus on abortion.

'I wanted to make sure that she could talk to me about it – her pain, her guilt . . .'

52

> 'Guilt?'
>
> 'Well, of course, it's a very self-destructive action, the ultimate self-harm.'
>
> 'I am not following you . . .' says the supervisor, who notices a raising heartbeat. She wants to butt in; she feels an urge to 'tell' Liza about her own beliefs around abortion, which are based on feminist theory. She recognises that they are about to embark on a conflict around basic beliefs so she pulls herself back and asks:
>
> 'How do you normally look at therapy? What do you see therapy as?'
>
> 'I suppose I want to give people the space to explore themselves, to come to their own conclusions about things . . .'
>
> 'What space did your client have to come to her own conclusions? The conclusions about abortion sounded pretty set to me.'
>
> Liza nods as a double-loop thinking on her intervention is beginning to take shape.

ACTIVITY 2.2

We all have cultural blind spots. You are invited to explore yours.

- Identify at least three different scenarios where your cultural values may clash with your client's values during their first interview.
- Take some time to consider how your views may affect your 'theory-in-use'. Some prompts, if needed, may be issues surrounding marriage and divorce, abortion, sexual identity or thoughts about sex change or arranged marriage, for example.
- Choose one of the examples where your own values might clash with those of your client's.
- Consider how your views may affect your 'theory-in-use'.
- If in a group, divide into pairs and exchange stories.

UNDERSTANDING 'WITH' OR 'ABOUT' – OR BOTH?

Casement (2008, p3) concludes that *there is a myth that the experienced therapist understands the patient swiftly and unerringly* and *this creates a pressure to know in order to be competent.* Casement (2008, p4) approaches 'knowing' in a fluid, dynamic sense and suggests that insights about the client rest on the unique, and *can be discovered afresh with each new patient.*

But can we fully step into another person's perspective? Carl Rogers (1961) argued that we can, and this has become an important cornerstone in person-centred theory. Rogers distinguished between understanding *with* the person versus *about* the person:

> *[U]nderstanding with a person, not about him is such an effective approach that it can bring about major changes. [I]t means to see the expressed ideas and attitudes from the other person's point of view, to sense how it feels to him, achieve his frame of reference to the things he is talking about.*
>
> (1961, p226)

However, Schön (1983) proposes that we inevitably always bring our own understanding into the equation, and the theory of reflective practice is concerned with making this as explicit as possible. This does not exclude the aim of stepping into another's shoes, but it draws our attention to our own footprints. The assessment addressed earlier with reference to Bateman and Holmes's (2002) idea about 'two strands' in an assessment implies that we understand both *with* and *about* the client. It reflects what the philosopher Ricoeur (1998) called dialectics between opposing viewpoints, which, when pitted against each other, can move our understanding forward. Ricoeur, like Schön, suggested that we always bring some kind of pre-understanding into the equation, which we should aim to let go of occasionally and try to surrender to the other's perspective. It is through this 'surrendering' that we learn with someone; we see the world from their eyes and aim to stand in the other person's shoes. However, in order to make sense of that experience we need to pull back and explore our experience with reference to a familiar frame of understanding, for example, a psychoanalytic, feminist or intercultural theory. These frameworks highlight different aspects and refer to the same experience but in different ways, depending on how one selects and analyses the information.

We can, suggests Ricoeur, move between what the neo-Kantian philosopher Dilthey called *Verstehen*, which stands for understanding, and *Erklärung*, which involves explaining. *Verstehen* happens when we immerse ourselves in someone else's perspective. *Erklärung* involves a distance equivalent to a natural scientific explanation where we group things together and focus on common factors or themes. Greenberg et al. (2003, p14) translate *Verstehen* and *Erklärung* into empathic understanding and causal explanation. Marquis (2008) explores different ways of approaching clients in assessment specifically. He uses the terms 'ideographic' and 'nomothetic'. 'Nomothetic' comes from the Greek *nomos*, which means 'law', and concerns categories and shared traits between people. An ideographic assessment in therapy reflects the phenomenological focus addressed earlier and emphasises the individual and unique. The term 'ideographic' originates from the Greek word *idios* meaning 'private' or 'own' and focuses on the unique traits of individuals. With parallels to Ricoeur, Marquis (2008) asserts that we need both types of understandings in our assessments.

EPISTEMOLOGY AND THE BASIC BELIEFS FROM WHICH WE DRAW EVIDENCE

The term in philosophy that concerns the issue of how we form any kind of knowledge about life and the world is called epistemology. *Verstehen*-thinking takes the epistemological stance that what we call reality rests on our own and others' understanding of it. *Erklärung* rests on the basic belief that there are fixed truths already there, regardless of the individual's beliefs.

In an extreme way, we can say that Liza confused *Verstehen* for *Erklärung*. She felt that she came across a 'truth' that explained both her client's situation and women's experiences of abortion in general. It is important to start in the client's understanding and try out different causal explanations for that, rather than trying to make the client's experience fit in with the explanation that we have at hand – as in the case of Liza.

> **REFLECTION POINT**
>
> - Liza breaks several ethical guidelines during her assessment interview. Which ones?

Keeping an open mind is essential so that we allow situations *to talk back at us* (Schön, 1983) and so that we can be sensitive to contraindications to our interpretations. We will return to this area. In our chapter about 'treatments', we shall look at 'truths' in terms of what Hinshelwood (1995) refers to as 'markers' that guide us through the untidy landscape of emotions and personal experiences.

> **KEY CONCEPTS**   Epistemology
>
> Epistemology comes from the ancient Greek words *episteme* meaning 'knowledge' and *logos* meaning 'rational'. Epistemology is largely concerned with breaking down the ladder of beliefs to get to the core of what we call knowledge. Epistemology asks questions about what we hold as 'evidence' (Cardinal et al, 2004, p11) and suggests that all knowledge is reached by 'inference' from one set of beliefs to another. Epistemology traces the ultimate foundation for belief and explores different ways of generating knowledge and validation.

ASSESSING RISK

We have looked at assessment in terms of combining an empathic understanding of the individual experience with a focus on themes and causal explanations. Sometimes, there are circumstances that prevent us from the empathic attempt to enter our client's experiences. There are all sorts of reasons why we cannot assess a client in the way we would ideally choose to do so. In the case study below, Shiri is taken aback and surprised, and has to consider her own safety. Themes and categories about risk and safety are important to her when forming a hypothesis about further treatment. Read the case study below and be prepared to document your reactions to her way of handling the situation with Jake. How would you act?

Case study 2.4

Shiri is expecting a couple who have booked an appointment over the phone through the husband, Mr Stephens. Shiri is a couple counsellor who has worked from home in a leafy suburb outside Birmingham for over 12 years. She advertises her couple work in *Yellow Pages* and on a website that clearly states that she works only with couples, not individuals, since her expertise is in communication patterns and ways of interacting. Assessment is an important part of her practice; she makes a point of discussing different options with her clients and works within a referral network of other therapists who specialise in areas such as psychosexual problems or individual short- or long-term therapy. These private practitioners have agreed on some common guidelines for their first assessments. Included in these considerations are referral options relating to medical as well as psychiatric care.

At the beginning of her career, Shiri agreed with some other therapists to 'look out for each other'. Before and after meeting new clients, she used to call her colleague Erica, in particular, who lives nearby. With time, she has gained confidence and faith in both her own ability and the ability of her clients to communicate and address issues. When Mr Stephens called, her ears pricked up at the sound of his voice; it had a kind of impatience and arrogance about it. There was a sense of urgency; Mr Stephens wanted an appointment immediately and sounded offended when the couple had to wait for the next available slot in ten days' time.

When the doorbell rings, Shiri is expecting a couple and is taken back when she finds only a man in his late thirties towering over her on the doorstep.

'Hi, I'm Jake', says the man, and makes a move towards the door. It crosses Shiri's mind that no one will hear her if she needs help. She reverses into the hallway and shows the man into the room. She beckons him to the chair that she usually sits in, furthest into the room. She leaves the door ajar.

'I am wondering if there has been a mistake', she says, still standing up. The man has already taken a seat. He seems restless and rocks back and forth in Shiri's chair.

'I was expecting a couple', she says.

'Yes, so was I! Believe me, so was I!' says Jake. 'Don't get me started. There no fucking limit to what she's up to, pardon my French, but this is not unusual, let me just tell you that!'

Jake talks for five minutes without stopping about the shortcomings of his wife. Shiri has sat down, but remains on the edge of her chair with a hand on each knee, and keeps her face straight as he speaks. Their eyes meet a couple of times, but she notices that Jake raises his voice at these moments; it seems to agitate him further rather than calming him down. When Jake pauses to catch his breath, Shiri breaks in, and speaks slowly and softly.

'This sounds very difficult for you both. It sounds to me as if it must be very hard to be in a relationship where you feel so distant and far away from each other.'

Jake nods.

'Therapy can be very helpful in these kind of situations,' continues Shiri 'but I think that we need to establish some ground rules from the beginning. A first consultation like this is not therapy as such, it is an opportunity to discuss expectations.'

Jake seems to relax; he listens.

'Now, one thing to reiterate from our telephone conversation is that I offer therapy for couples. I work with patterns of communication and interaction within relationships.'

Shiri moves on to explain different options with the help of her questionnaire, which she introduces to Jake as her 'first consultation questionnaire', and they go through it together.

'This also includes exploring options and considering referrals for individual therapy or maybe medical care,' she explains.

When addressing the question about previous medical treatment, Jake discloses that he has been advised by his GP to 'look into his anger management issues'. Jake explains to Shiri that he has got high blood pressure and diabetes and that 'getting angry doesn't help'.

Shiri is reminded of Aveline's words that to *maintain and reinforce [the client's] defence is the best choice* (1997, p110). She recognises that she is not in the best position to help Jake to explore his situation freely, given her concern for her own safety and her inability to 'hold' Jake in her private practice.

She decides to focus on tangible goals, such as Jake's blood pressure and diabetes, which she suggests can be linked to his mood swings. She advises him to return to his GP, and also provides Jake with a leaflet about the local NHS clinic where he could get a psychiatric assessment, via GP referral, and be offered either CBT, long-term psychotherapy or family therapy depending on his needs. As he leaves, Jake agrees to focus on his own reactions and inner resources, rather than putting all responsibilities on to his wife. He says he would like return to his GP to discuss his blood pressure although he is not sure about that there is any point in discussing mood swings or a referral to the NHS clinic.

COMMENT

Aveline stresses the importance of insight into our own limitations when assessing a client in private practice:

If the counsellor is assessing for his or her own practice, the key question is: do I have sufficient time, interest and relevant skills for the therapy of this client? If not, who has?

(1997, p113)

Case study 2.4 illustrates how sometimes as therapists we are thrown by a situation. Shiri's reflection revolved primarily around emotions in the room, and she feels afterwards that she acted largely on impulse. She sits down with a piece of paper and begins to structure her thoughts and feelings, as a means of preparing for her next supervision session.

Her reason for not offering Jake further therapy was legitimised by the fact that she offers therapy only to couples. She feels at the same time that she has tried to take into account both Jake's and her own interests. The way they approached referral options felt congruent with the principles addressed by Aveline about referrals. It also resonated with Aveline's (1997, p133) suggestion to *work from simpler problems to the more complex* with respect for the client's defences. Based on both actions and Jake's own account of the problems with his wife, he may not have been able to 'hold' both intrapsychic and interpersonal conflicts at this stage. The fact that he had ignored Shiri's insistence that she only sees couples was significant.

Still, Shiri takes some time to double-loop her actions. Was she being fair to Jake? Would she have felt more safe if he was older, built differently or had been a woman? As Strean would have put it, did Jake remind Shiri of someone from her own past? On what basis had she assessed him as a risk? To what extent had her assessment of Jake been ethically sound?

Another ethical concern that Shiri wants to discuss with her supervisor relates to Jake's wife. Should she perhaps take some form of action? She feels unsettled and uneasy after the first meeting with Jake and decides to call a member of her supervision group to ground herself. She also decides to call her supervisor to discuss the option of an earlier appointment.

RISK ASSESSMENT

We will return to the issue of risk assessment in the section on assessment in organisations. In private practice, being alone raises additional concerns for safety. Despenser (2007) found that many therapists express concern about their vulnerability. When asked about what factors the therapist would take into account during their assessment with regard to their own safety, most therapists, regardless of their modality, referred to 'gut reaction', 'all antennae active' and 'instincts' (Despenser 2007, p14).

A. Assessing the client's current state
1. Presenting state *Hostile? Agitated? Vengeful? Paranoid? Attitude to violence? Insight into own contribution to trigger situation? Attitude to help, including therapy?*
2. Threatened/planned violence *Threats? Identified targets? Actual plans?*
3. Current circumstances *Threats to self-image? Recent changes and removals of safety net?*
4. Resources *Social network? Enough stability? How else can trigger situations be managed? Willingness to collaborate with therapist?*
B. Taking the client's history
1. History of violence *Incidents, age, frequency, severity, weapons, sexual offences, cruelty to animals?*
2. Behaviour and characteristics *Degree of self-control? Isolation, communication skills?* *Coping and problem-solving skills? Lack of guilt or concern?*
C. Background
1. Psychiatric/medical *Psychotic symptoms? Addictions? Medical conditions that destabilise mood?*
2. Socio-demographic *Male? Young? Low educational achievement? Rootless? Restless? Experiences of institutions?*

Table 2.1: Assessing the risk for violence

Source: adapted from Despenser 2007.

'DIAGNOSING' PROBLEMS

Despenser divides the factors that therapists reported they would take into account during an assessment into three categories.

- Signposts in the client's history, such as reported use of medication, episodes of violence, aggression, abuse and psychiatric or forensic history.
- Signposts in the client's current state, including evidence of an erratic state, intoxication, body language, verbal clues and recent or anticipated changes in the client's situation or support network.
- Clues in countertransference feelings, from first hearing the client's voice to feelings occurring throughout the work.

Shiri felt cautious about addressing her client's anger in the room. Addressing his feelings with reference to blood pressure, diabetes and mood swings felt less confrontational and more manageable for Jake to digest.

ACTIVITY 2.3

Take some time to consider some of the risk assessment issues addressed in Table 2.1.

- To what extent do you consider that Shiri's actions were informed by risk assessments?
- What do you think that she did right and what could she have done differently, taking into account your own modality and experience?

REFERRALS

Daines et al. argue that it is important for private practitioners to know where to turn in case of medical, psychiatric or social care related advice or referrals. They write:

> *The counsellor cannot operate with the knowledge base and expertise of a psychiatrist or GP, but needs to be able to form a credible judgement about whether a recommendation or referral to see a medical practitioner is needed.*
> (2007, p28)

We need to feel safe in order to practise. Daines et al. remind us about taking the conditions of private practitioners into consideration when we consider referrals:

> *In some instances the work setting of the counsellor may be the key factor in deciding whether the person can be seen. Those who . . . can call on immediate help if personal safety is threatened may be in a position to*

consider referrals that those working in a more isolated or less well-staffed setting may not.

(2007, p27)

There is, in this sense, always a reality out there that needs to be considered when we assess therapeutic practice with reference to ethical guidelines.

CONFLICTS BETWEEN GUIDELINES

Jenkins (2007) highlights how there is often a conflict between guidelines. In Shiri's case the principle of self-care may need to be balanced with the guidelines for beneficence, i.e. the work has to actively benefit the client. Another difficult juncture can sometimes occur during the assessment when the interests of a third person come into the picture. How do we deal with the ethical guidelines about fidelity, confidentiality and autonomy when we believe someone, the client included, may be at serious risk of harm? Jenkins writes:

[K]ey ethical principles, perhaps those regarding client autonomy and avoiding harm, may be in conflict. This may happen with regard to the issue of preventing suicide, or avoiding harm intended by a client towards third party.

(2007, p127)

Jenkins stresses two points for consideration.

- Act in accordance with a relevant code of practice and seek professional consultation or supervision regarding the issue.
- Restrict disclosure to contacts most relevant to the issue and those best *able to act in the public interest.*

The ethical framework involves a distinction between areas where the therapist *may* break and *must* break confidentiality.

The therapist *may* break confidentiality on the basis of it being in the public interest when reporting:

- a crime;
- malpractice;
- suspected child abuse;
- suspected suicide;
- professional misconduct.

We *must* break confidentiality in the case of:

- a suspected terrorist attack.

ACTIVITY 2.4

- Consider which people or agencies you could add to your support network in case of emergency.

If you experience a lack of a support network, please consider the following steps.

- Gather contact details for your local GP, psychiatric resources, social services, drug treatment centres, etc.
- Prepare to discuss your list of contacts with your supervisor. Discuss the merits of contacting the agencies on your list, to introduce yourself and describe your own services.
- Read, discuss and consider the implications of the contacts list. Jenkins (2007) and Mitchels and Bond (2010) offer accessible advice on the potential implications surrounding confidentiality and other ethical issues.

CHAPTER SUMMARY

This chapter has revolved around 'diagnosing' problems and making a 'hypothesis' about the client's needs and possible further treatment. Risk assessment, including the element of surprise, has been referred to as part of this process. Making a hypothesis has been explored with consideration to some of the following aspects.

- Diagnosis and formulation can sometimes be conflicting concepts. In this chapter we have explored diagnosing in terms of 'sieving' for common themes and patterns.
- The concept of formulation captures the importance of being sensitive to client feedback. 'Hypotheses' are collaborative and ongoing concerns. Our evidence for a hypothesis comes, as Hinshelwood (1995, p156) asserts, from the client's response: *the response to an interpretation is . . . the criterion for deciding whether to retain the hypothesis or abandon it.*
- We have considered the option of understanding both *with* and *about* the client, in light of openness to the unique combined with a focus on themes.
- The issue of 'practising what we preach' is explored with reference to Schön and Argyris's distinction between an 'espoused theory' and a 'theory-in-use'. Sometimes we are not aware of the differences between what we say and what we do, as in the case study with Liza

who worked with a person-centred theory in mind but imposed her values about anti-abortion on the client at the same time.
- Ethical guidelines can sometimes collide. Different interests have to be weighed up carefully, particularly with regard to guidelines about confidentiality and doing no harm.

SUGGESTED FURTHER READING

Daines, B, Gask, L and Howes, A (2007) *Medical and psychiatric issues for counsellors.* Professional Skills for Counsellors series. London: Sage.

This is another accessible book about psychiatric and medical conditions, with advice on how to recognise mental health problems and how to deal with safety, referrals and ethical problems.

Jenkins, P (2007) *Counselling, psychotherapy and the law.* London: Sage.

This book is an invaluable source of reference for issues relating to law and ethical guidelines in therapeutic practice. Jenkins writes in an interesting and stimulating way about ethical solutions to a wide range of dilemmas.

Some particularly relevant BACP information sheets are:

Freet, R (2008) *P8 – Psychopharmacology and counselling and psychotherapy.* Lutterworth: BACP.

Peden, A (2010) *G18 – Recognising and acting upon child sexual abuse.* Lutterworth: BACP

Reeves, A and Seber, P (2007) *P7 – Working with the suicidal client.* Lutterworth: BACP.

Walley, S (2008) *P17 – Making referrals.* Lutterworth: BACP.

CHAPTER 3

Treatment – illuminating shaded areas?

> **CORE KNOWLEDGE**
>
> What can we hope to offer our clients in private practice in terms of treatment? This chapter focuses on the differences between and overlapping features within different modalities.
>
> - We will pursue Hinshelwood's thinking on hypotheses as an ongoing attempt to put out 'markers' as means of *recognising the currents in the interaction that pull or push* the therapist.
> - The issue of 'markers' will be assessed alongside the core modalities. What are the differences and similarities between the different models? What guides the therapist and the client through the different types of therapeutic processes or journeys?
> - We will return to the issue of the therapist as a person with a case study that revisits key themes such as countertransference and double-loop thinking. The issues of self-care and how to avoid the 'rescuing trap' will be looked at in greater depth.

So, what happens next? What do we actually offer our clients after the first interview? Well, it varies.

OFFERING AN INFORMED, PROFESSIONAL SERVICE

Being realistic about what we can offer is naturally carried through into an ongoing treatment plan. The sooner clients discover their own strength in therapy the better, and an overriding purpose of all schools of counselling and psychotherapy is to facilitate the client in their discovery of latent strengths. This often happens through reassessing the meanings they have so far attached to events, experiences and relationships. Bion captures this thinking in his reference to past events:

The reason why we concern ourselves with things that are remembered and with our past history, is not because of what it was . . . but because of the mark it has left on you or me or us, now.

(1962, p38)

Many therapists may agree that therapy involves a collaborative process towards throwing light on previously shaded meanings. But just how to go about this is often a cause for debate between, and within, the different theoretical frameworks.

SOME DIFFERENT WAYS OF CO-CREATING MEANINGS

The typical psychodynamic therapist approaches the issue of attaching ('illuminating') new meanings to events and experiences with reference to the 'unconscious'. The 'unconscious' originally referred to an entity or a 'thing', as can be seen in Freud's battle with his contemporaries in medical science. It is nowadays often used as a metaphor for affective meanings of which we are unaware. Bateman and Holmes illustrate the shift in the way the term 'unconscious' is used today:

With the shift in contemporary psychoanalysis away from mechanism towards meaning, 'the unconscious' becomes a metaphor for the affective meanings of which the patient is unaware of, and which emerges through the relationship with the analyst. 'Unconscious' becomes an adjective rather than a noun.

(2002, p29)

Earlier, we referred to the psychoanalytically inspired concept of the 'point of maximum pain'. It is a key concept in Hinshelwood's (1995) theory about assessing the client in three ways. Hinshelwood writes:

Clinical material is best approached as pictures of relationships with objects. There are then three areas of object relationships which I try to bear in mind.

1. *The current life situation.*
2. *The infantile object relations, as described in the patient's history, or hypothesised from what is known.*
3. *The relationship with the assessor which, to all intents and purposes is the beginning of a transference.*

(1995, p157)

An existential therapist would perhaps object to the focus on the past. *Deep*, writes Yalom does not have to mean *early*:

> *To Freud, exploration always meant excavation . . . Deepest conflict means earliest conflict . . . To explore deeply from an existential perspective does not mean that one explores the past; rather, it means that one brushes away everyday concerns and thinks deeply about one's existential situation.*
>
> (1980, pp11–12)

Death, freedom, isolation and meaninglessness are four fundamental transpersonal concerns that can be said to *cut beneath any individual's personal life history* and *constitute the corpus of existential psychodynamics* (Yalom, 1980, p10).

The existential therapist would aim for what Buber coined an I–Thou relationship. It is an open, present and mutual relationship (Friedman, 1999), or what Clarksson (1995) calls a *person-to-person* relationship where the practitioner aims towards 'being with' rather than 'doing to' the client. The existential therapist would, typically, contrast the psychodynamic formulation with an attempt to 'bracket' themselves; the therapist would aim to put aside prior understandings and meet the client *with an attitude of wonder that will allow the specific circumstances and experiences to unfold in their own right* (Spinelli, 1997). It is the 'not knowing' that existential therapy is focused on. Existentialism rests on the assumption that there is no ultimate knowing; life lacks a preordained design. We are subsequently *condemned to freedom*, which makes each of us ultimately responsible for the meaning of our own life; van Deurzen emphasises the *complete openness* required by therapists. But, just like their psychodynamic colleagues, existential therapists are guided by some categories that reflect their pre-understanding about *what to look out for*:

> *The existential counsellor or therapist needs to come to the sessions with complete openness to the individual situation and with an attitude of wonder that will allow the specific circumstances and experiences to unfold in their own right. Assisting other human beings in understanding their own life in a genuine and meaningful manner is a serious matter. Each and every discovery is personal and unpredictable. We can, however, distinguish a number of themes that will often emerge in this process.*
>
> (van Deurzen, 2009)

An existential therapist is likely to look out for signs of the client's experience of human conditions or 'givens'. Like the psychodynamic therapist, the existential therapist has a repertoire of categories to serve as landmarks. They may look for expressions of self-deception or 'bad faith' in response to 'existential anxiety' when faced with 'situated freedom'. Existential therapy distances itself from the idea of 'regressing' and re-experiencing previous relationships to achieve change and seeks to enter into the subjective experience of the client. Yalom writes:

> *The ... existential analyst must approach the patient's phenomenology; that is, he or she must enter the patient's experiential world.*
>
> (1980, p17)

Existentialism thus emphasises how all are born with the view of dying and with the personal responsibility of finding a meaning to a life to which no preordained design is offered. However, in a similar way to their psychodynamic colleagues, the existentialists propose that some bring unhelpful templates into therapy that, as addressed by van Deurzen in the quote above, become themes in the therapeutic process. Similar to psychodynamic thinking, existential therapy assumes that some may suffer more than necessary due to a defence gone wrong. At some stage, the client may have adapted a stance to his or her reality that at one time promised some form of protection. Yalom writes:

> *[A]ll human beings are in a quandary, but some are unable to cope with it; psychopathology depends not merely on the presence or the absence of stress but on the interaction between ubiquitous stress and the individual's mechanism of defence.*
>
> (1980, p13)

All practitioners, argues Schön (Schön, 1983; Schön and Rein, 1994) frame their understandings. Framing one's understanding does not make the practitioner a non-reflective practitioner. The main thing, asserts Schön, is that we aim to know how and why we frame, or as Hinshelwood (1995) would put it, follow certain 'markers'. In the end, asserts Hinshelwood, our ongoing formulations of hypotheses are markers that are tentatively positioned while taking into account the client's response. Hinshelwood (1995, p156) emphasises that we cannot validate our hypotheses or build up evidence as is the case in the natural or medical sciences. He writes:

> *[A]ny hypothesis is in my own mind a marker of where I am in the material, of finding bearings, of recognising the currents in the interaction that pull or push me.*

The person-centred therapist may work with the idea of an 'organismic self'. The 'treatment plan', if such a concept were used in person-centred practice, revolves around self-actualisation and internalised locus of evaluation. At the core of person-centred therapy rests the belief that each of us has an inherent capacity for self-understanding and change, a propensity for self-actualisation. With this in mind, the therapist aims to facilitate appropriate conditions for the client to develop, through 'core conditions' in terms of empathy, unconditional positive regard, congruence and realness. The healing process rests on a relationship between the therapist and client based on genuine, empathic and caring non-verbal and verbal behaviour.

The cognitive-behavioural therapist, on the other hand, aims to increase awareness through cognitive changes. A key concept for cognitive-behavioural therapists is 'metacognition', which captures the way we reflect, deconstruct and understand our own cognitive processes. While the psychodynamic therapist may regard transference as a 'place' to connect unconscious and conscious awareness, the cognitive-behavioural therapist may perceive 'metacognition' as where awareness can be reached. While a psychodynamic therapist may conceptualise unhelpful templates for processing new information in terms of 'object relations', 'splitting' or 'ego strength', a cognitive behavioural therapist may conceptualise awareness as a process reached via 'automatic thoughts', 'cognitive distortions' and 'cognitive schemata' with the view of highlighting core beliefs as potentially unhelpful templates for processing new information.

Case study 3.1

Claire is an experienced counsellor who usually assesses her clients on a number of set themes. They range from the client's presenting problems to their history and ability to relate to the therapist. Claire has been ambivalent about taking on more clients at the moment due to her substantial case load, but she reports in supervision that she is satisfied with taking on Hannah, a 35-year-old mother of two. In fact, she has agreed to do so for a fee that is £15 below her average fee despite knowing that Hannah can afford private education for her three children.

'She seemed so motivated, you know – prepared to really deal with her problems,' says Claire.

'That sounds good,' answers her supervisor. 'I'm just not really clear about why you took on another client in spite of feeling over worked . . . and why you did so for a reduced fee.'

Claire looks unhappy.

'To be honest, I've been wondering that myself.'

The supervisor remains silent. Claire looks pensive.

'I think that I was taken aback . . . She wasn't what I had expected. She was so . . . well, stunning.'

Claire shifts uneasily in her chair, and continues.

'She looked like Elle Macpherson. You know, the model that they call The Body. Tall, slim . . . and so gentle, softly spoken, well mannered and all that.'

'How did that make you feel?' asks the supervisor.

'Well . . . clumsy, fat . . . boring.'

Claire sighs and adds:

'And that's nothing new. It's like I'm in school again, trying to be with the cheerleaders . . .'

The supervisor remains silent while Claire seems lost in thought. Eventually she continues:

> 'Then she started crying. It reminded me that this was an assessment and yet I found myself asking questions as if we were already in therapy. I think it made her open up too soon and too quickly. I didn't get much information about her really, not much background. It became more about . . . well, about connecting, perhaps?'
>
> 'How did her crying affect you?'
>
> Claire shakes her head and says 'It made me feel useful . . . valuable . . .'
>
> 'Less boring?'
>
> 'I'm afraid so . . .'
>
> 'And what about Hannah's presented problem?'
>
> 'She felt that her life lacked direction . . . she talked about having been raised to be a pretty wife, you know, went to finishing school in Switzerland and all that . . .'
>
> 'So, always pleasing others was part of her presented problem?'
>
> Claire nods. Together with her supervisor she begins to explore what Hannah might have projected in terms of her own values, while unpicking how her own material played a part in the unexpected outcome of the assessment session.
>
> They agree that it is an experience that Claire can use – 'recycle' – in the therapy with Hannah. Claire is hopeful about being able to use this experience to facilitate Hannah's own understanding of herself and how she is met in the world, feeling stuck in a rut of 'aiming to please'.

REFLECTION POINT

- After reading Case study 3.1, consider how events could be explored differently perhaps through a different modality.

COMMENT

The case study with Claire revisits some of the issues addressed earlier, in terms of the twin principles in private practice of 'doing no harm' and being realistic about what one is capable of and prepared to offer. How will this client affect you? What impact may this work have on you and your family? The difficulty for many of us often lies in saying 'no'. Quite often this difficulty taps into a complex pattern for 'helpers' and, if unattended, it can have serious effects on further treatment. In this section, the issue highlighted in the case study about 'helping' will be approached with reference to how our own 'shadows' and 'hooks' can make us susceptible to the 'rescuing trap'.

The case study with Claire and Hannah also illustrates how the client's and the therapist's material can mix right from the start. If Claire is to continue her work with Hannah on the basis that Hannah will be an engaging, hard-working 'damsel in distress' who lends herself as someone for Claire to 'rescue', the assessment could be said to have gone wrong. Reflective practice takes into account the fact that all professionals are human and stresses the importance of daring to address one's errors, rather than shunning, denying and maybe displacing them or acting them out in the work. For Claire, an important learning experience opens up with regard to her own 'hook' or 'shadow'.

If explored within a psychodynamically inspired framework, Hannah may, on the one hand, be said to be 'projecting' her own image of herself as someone whose self-worth relies on pleasing others. Projective identification usually refers to 'disowned' and unwanted emotions – emotions that we have learnt to perceive as unacceptable. To be pleasant and attractive could be a side of Hannah that she has learnt to try to disown, and it may be because of this very dilemma that her life lacks direction and meaning. When exploring her own reactions in supervision, Claire acknowledges that she too has engaged in a personally familiar drama. Hannah has hooked into something personal. Claire has, in spite of promising herself not to, too readily jumped into a familiar 'carer' role. We spoke earlier of two types of countertransference: one that, simply speaking, stems from the client and one that taps into the therapist's issues. The former is considered as 'projected' by the client and is referred to by Cashdan:

> *[with projective identification] it is as if one individual forces another to play a role in the enactment of that person's internal drama – one involving early object relationships.*
>
> (1988, p56)

Projective identification is usually referred to in terms of a *patient-derived countertransference* (Bateman and Holmes, 2002, p85) where *the analyst's experiences are a direct result of what the patient is 'putting into' him*. In this case, however, Claire and her supervisor gradually unravel how Claire's own lapses in confidence and her entrenched pattern of seeking approval through 'being there for others' come into play.

As Sedgwick puts it, it is important to consider how *the carrier of projection is not just any object . . . but someone who offers a 'hook' to hang on* (1994, p112). Double-loop learning suggests that we transform our mistakes into learning experiences. The considerations given to how our own interpretations may be diluted by our own biases and blind spots is an ongoing concern and something that we cannot free ourselves from entirely. Sedgwick (1994, p112) adopts the stance that the therapist *needs not to eliminate his pathology but know it and utilise it.*

> ## ACTIVITY 3.1
>
> Claire based her understanding of events on some psychoanalytical principles about projective identification and countertransference.
>
> - Would you have viewed the case differently? Review events with another modality in mind. How could the situation be used in therapy, from your point of view?

SO, WHO 'KNOWS' BEST?

Nobody does. Although there are themes and common patterns between people and their problems, every client and the 'truth' derived from them can, as suggested earlier, be regarded as relatively unique. The only way of 'knowing' is usually by rendering what is available and accessible at the time and to do so with an openness to the client's reactions and progress.

The markers are intuitive hypotheses that are to be 'tried out *with*' the client, rather than 'tried out *on*'. We are, after all, suggests Hinshelwood (1995, p156), trying *to think when under fire* (Bion, cited in Hinshelwood, 1995, p156) and need to be prepared to reconsider our conclusions on an ongoing basis.

Bion (1962) strongly opposed any 'rights' or 'wrongs'. Like Hinshelwood, he considered the proof to be in the pudding. A hypothesis is only true as long as the client experiences it as valid. Bion writes:

> *In psychoanalytical methodology the criterion cannot be whether a particular usage is right or wrong, meaningful or verifiable, but whether it does or does not promote development.*
>
> (1962, p7)

Bion also suggested that the therapist should enter each session *without memory and desire*. At the same time, however, 'framing' could be said to be at the heart of Bion's practice. He understood the challenge for humans of 'learning how to think for oneself'. 'How do I become my own subjective being?' was a key question raised by Bion. He implied that we more often than not see the world through the lenses of others, and the ability to find our own lenses, or outlook, on the world around us was an underlying theme in his theory. He conceptualised memories as *undigested facts*, which he labelled *beta-elements*. He compared the term 'alpha function' with the act of 'digestion' to describe the transformation of emotions into *personal possessions rather than facts* (1962, p35).

Bion adhered to British philosopher David Hume's assumption that 'cause' is something inferred by habit and previous experience. For instance, we expect that the sun will rise in the morning because we have frequently experienced sunrise and morning together. Hume described this as a constant conjunction rather than as a necessary connection (Hume, in Cardinal et al., 2000). If something follows an event frequently enough, our belief in this connection grows, and we are led to create a necessary connection in our minds. The event impresses itself upon our imagination and leads us to believe that the second event will follow. We begin to speak of the first event as 'causing' the second event, when in fact 'cause' is just a feature of human psychology.

Cognitive analytical therapy (CAT) is an example of an attempt to bridge psychoanalysis, person-centred therapy and cognitive behavioural therapy. The therapist adopts a congruent stance and invites the client to a highly interactive collaboration about core constructs, which may be revealed as values and beliefs rather than 'facts'.

The CAT model adheres to therapies that see *parallels between the process of childhood leaning and therapy* (Ryle and Kerr, 2002, p33), but object to the notion that 'deep' change depends on a process of regression and, consequently, transference. Ryle and Kerr write:

> *Therapeutic change is seen to depend on the creation of a non-collusive relationship with the patient informed by the joint creations of mediating tools such as letters and diagrams within a phased, time-limited relationship.*
>
> (2002, p33)

'No single methodology can do justice to the complexity of the human mind' writes Green (2003, p1), who contends that there is 'an integration between biology and psychoanalysis on the agenda'. Neuroscience can certainly help therapists to conceptualise many complex problems, and it is likely that the findings will lend us tools and concepts during both our first assessment and in ongoing 'treatment'.

INTEGRATION-IN-ACTION AND COMMON FACTOR THEORY

As suggested earlier, Argyris and Schön found that people often failed to implement their espoused theory (Argyris and Schön, 1978). One important finding in their research was that the absence of the espoused theory more often than not surprised the practitioners themselves. The reasons for the discrepancy between what we *say we do* and what we *actually do* are many, ranging from unconscious decisions to organisational, cultural factors that obscure the practitioner's own sight.

Holmes and Bateman (2002) suggest that sometimes the development of the espoused theory is a question of making a conscious decision to be theoretically agile enough to accommodate an openness for the unique. Such theoretical flexibility is linked to offering an integrative practice that is guided by the client's needs. In these cases we can talk about 'integration-in-practice' as a form of integrative method grown from 'reflection-in-practice' by experienced therapists (Holmes and Bateman, 2002, pp4–6).

Wosket addresses an emerging 'common factor paradigm' within evaluative research about therapy, asserting that:

> *[t]he idea that effective outcomes in counselling and psychotherapy are determined not by approach/specific strategies and procedures, but rather by common therapeutic factors across all schools is . . . now gaining ascendance.*
> (1999, p15)

Research indicates that it may not be a matter of one approach being more successful than the other but rather a question of how effective the therapist is in using the approach at hand (Wosket, 1999).

Green agrees with the common factor theory and identifies a 'post-tribal' trend in therapeutic practice:

> *I think that as a profession we have moved into a post-tribal phase, where we have learned that we have much more in common with each other than that which divides us . . . [A]t the heart of any successful counselling encounter is the quality of the therapeutic relationship, which is the working alliance formed between you, the counsellor, and your client . . . There must be real engagement between the two.*
> (Green, 2010, pp2, 4)

The common factor approach states that *therapies work because of what they have in common, rather than because of what differentiates them* (Hoffman and Weinberger, 2007, p104). Hoffman and Weinberger (2007, p107) assert that *the therapeutic relationship is, by far, the most written about common factor*, but they propose five common factors that *empirical data seem to support*.

1. *The therapeutic relationship* This is central to psychodynamic and humanistic/experiential approaches and *seems to be genuinely related to therapeutic success* across the modalities.
2. *Expectations of treatment effectiveness* What, in medical treatment, is called the placebo effect is *no less powerful in psychotherapeutic settings*. Expectancy has been noted in behavioural treatments in particular (Hoffman and Weinberg, 2003, p106f). By putting faith into the treatment and expecting progress, people feel better.

3. *Confronting or facing problems (exposure)* Cognitive therapy explicitly makes use of exposure to, for example, self-defeating verbalisations or pathogenic cognitions and beliefs that can then be altered. Psychoanalytic thinking rests on the belief that talking about upsetting or traumatic events has a positive effect. Humanistic/experiential theories also adhere to the belief that confronting or facing problems is beneficial.
4. *Mastery or control experiences* This is a central factor to the cognitive and behavioural approaches and *is relatively neglected by psychodynamic and humanistic/experiential thinkers* (Hoffman and Weinberger, 2007, p108). Psychodynamic thinkers rely on insights into desires, fears and defences that indirectly lead to mastery experiences. Most humanistic strands also adopt the view that mastery will unfold naturally and 'organically' as opposed to Beck's cognitive therapy which *explicitly fosters mastery experiences* (Hoffman and Weinberger, 2007, p108) through structured tasks and well-defined goals. Aaron Beck created the Beck Depression Inventory (BDI, BDI-II), which is a 21-question multiple-choice self-report inventory (Beck, 2006). It is a widely used instrument for measuring the severity of depression.
5. *Attribution of therapeutic outcome* While expectations of treatment are formed *before* therapy, 'attribution' is formed *during* therapy and concerns how the client understands and views progress. Attributing the outcomes of therapy to a wonderful therapist can, asserts Hoffman and Weinberger (2003, p116), cause the client to believe that positive change lies outside rather than within them. The treatment success is markedly higher in those cases where the client believes that positive change lies within them, for instance, in terms of changed coping skills and/or altered personality styles.

Psychological realities will always be 'messy', ambivalent and subject to change. The particular truths that we may hope to reach in therapy *do not have the property of extension or tangibility*, asserts Symington (1986, p17). Truth *cannot be measured but it does exist*.

> *Most psychological realities do not have the property of extension or tangibility; a dream, an hallucination, a belief, a thought. Truth is a reality of this nature. It cannot be measured but it does exist; the fact that it is difficult to define does not detract from this.*
>
> (1986, p17)

Each encounter with a client involves something totally new, given the complexity of each human being's meaning-making processes. Therapeutic practice is an ongoing journey through untidy landscapes, usually littered by what may come across as wasted experiences. The ethical principle about self-respect invites not only clients but also therapists to 'recycle' (Bager-

Charleson 2010a) our mistakes. It encourages us to capture the mistakes and use them for their transformative value, which springs from bringing experiences to personal therapy and supervision, and from putting our personal events in a context of ongoing literature, research or training. By constantly reassessing our 'markers' and being sensitive to contraindications with regard to our interpretations, we will always move within the span of *Verstehen* and *Erklärung*, striving for empathic understanding and sieving for themes. While we allow ourselves to move with, and be moved by, the client, both our theory and our selves will invariably expand and develop. Assessment is, in this sense, guided by a mixture of things. It requires clinical knowledge but also, as Johnstone and Dallos highlight, a great deal of reflexivity:

> *Reflexivity is central to good clinical formulation. By this we mean that our own assumptions, motives, cultural attitudes and interpretive lenses need to be transparent in order to ensure an open working formulation. Central to this is self-awareness.*
>
> (2006, p168)

CHAPTER SUMMARY

- This chapter has revolved around differences and overlapping features between 'treatment' models in counselling and psychotherapy.
- We have looked at concepts such as common factor theory and treatment models developed from 'integration-in-practice'.
- With examples from psychodynamic, existential, person-centred and cognitive behavioural theory, the basis for 'treatment' has been explored in the light of clinical knowledge in combination with reflexivity.

SUGGESTED FURTHER READING

Below are some 'classics' as well as some newer books, all referring to therapeutic practice in illuminating and inspiring ways.

Casement, P (1991) *Learning from the patient.* New York and London: Guilford Press.

This is an accessible account of psychoanalytically inspired work, in which Casement uses both his own and others' mistakes to illustrate what can happen in the consulting room.

Grant, A, Townend, M and Mill, J (2008) *Assessment and case formulation in cognitive behavioural therapy.* London: Sage.

This book gives a good insight into CBT practice and assessment. The authors write with reference to their own clinical work and illustrate how assessment and formulation evolve throughout the process. Their case examples include helping individuals with problems such as psychosis, depression, borderline personality disorder and family case formulation.

Lichner Ingram, B (2006) *Clinical case formulations: matching the integrative treatment plan to the client.* Hoboken, NJ: Wiley.

For those who wish to deepen their knowledge of assessment, this is an excellent source. Lichner Ingram approaches case formulations with a broad perspective on therapy, ranging from personal to cultural issues, which she illustrates with case studies.

Rogers, C (1961) *A therapist's view of psychotherapy.* London: Constable and Co.

This book captures Rogers's outlook on life and his therapeutic practice. It gives an insightful and compelling account of therapeutic practice with reference to philosophy as well as practical advice.

Rowan, J and Jacobs, M (2003) *The therapist's use of self.* Maidenhead: Open University Press.

Rowan and Jacobs explore therapy from different angles, Rowan being anchored in person-centred thinking and Jacobs drawing from his expertise as a psychoanalytic therapist. Together they find common ground and suggest that we look at differences within therapeutic practice in the light of the therapist's different beliefs, values and 'notions of self', rather than seeing them as issues of different modalities.

Yalom, I (1991) *Love's executioner.* London and New York: Penguin.

This is a moving and easy-to-read account of therapy where Yalom is present both as a person and a practitioner. Through eight case studies Yalom takes us on a journey filled with insightful observations from an existential as well as a simply human point of view.

CHAPTER 4

Assessment in organisations: an overview

> **CORE KNOWLEDGE**
>
> In this chapter we will:
>
> - review the concepts of transference, contracts, reflective practice and ethics and reflect on them from the perspective of clinical assessment in organisations;
> - provide an overview of organisations offering out-patient psychological therapies;
> - explore two of the assessment methods used in organisations.
>   1. Telephone assessment.
>   2. Face-to-face assessment.

INTRODUCTION

This chapter focuses on assessments for counselling and psychotherapy in organisations. We will revisit the key assessment concepts from the organisational perspective, introduce statutory and non-statutory organisations that offer outpatient counselling and reflect on the main methods of assessment used by them.

In her chapters on assessments in private practice, Sofie has covered a number of key concepts and principles used in assessment that are common to both private practice and organisations. I will therefore refer to them only briefly to avoid repetition.

THE 'THIRD' IN THE RELATIONSHIP: TRANSFERENCE AND COUNTERTRANSFERENCE

In Chapter 2 Sofie explored the concepts of transference and countertransference within an assessment session, and quoted the following definition of transference:

> *Transference refers to the ways in which the feelings, wishes, and actions of the patient in relation to the therapist may be unconsciously influenced, coloured, and distorted by earlier childhood experiences, especially those with parents.*
>
> Holmes and Lindley (1998, p126)

The same process emerges within an organisational assessment, whether the assessment happens face-to-face or by telephone. An organisational setting itself provides another opportunity for transference to take place and I refer to it as 'a third' in the assessment relationship.

Case study 4.1

Jane is a woman in her fifties. She has been unemployed for some months and struggles to make ends meet. Jane lives in a council flat in a busy, deprived area of the town. She has been diagnosed with depression and her GP has suggested counselling at the low-cost clinic. She has made an appointment for an assessment.

The counselling service is based in a large Victorian building that also houses the training institute. It is in a green, leafy neighbourhood with big houses surrounding the park. The waiting area is busy with staff and students bustling around. Jane sits down in the comfortable leather armchair and waits for the assessor. The assessor is a woman who looks a lot younger than her, smartly dressed and friendly. She takes her into the room. This is a large, bright room with big comfortable armchairs and sofas.

Jane sits down in one of them and feels very small. She is very uneasy about being here and feels that she doesn't belong. She feels a sense of shame about bringing her unhappy life to this place and wants to run away. She starts 'I hope I'm not wasting your time . . .'

ACTIVITY 4.1

Take some time to consider the following.

- What do you think may have been evoked for Jane by coming to this service? What do you think she may need to help her stay in the assessment?
- Reflect on the organisation where you work. What sort of transferential response might it evoke in clients? Consider issues of context and difference such as class, culture, disability.

COMMENT

In this case study we are examining the role of social context in how the client experiences the service. Similar issues might arise with differences such as ethnicity, age, disability and gender.

CONTRACTS

Sofie has explored contracts in depth in Chapter 1. Contracts are also one of the core principles in transactional analysis, based on the assumption that both the therapist and the client are responsible human beings, capable of making agreements about the business aspects as well as the aims of therapy.

Berne (1966) referred to three different areas of contract: administrative (or business contracts); professional (agreements about the focus of counselling and how it will occur); and psychological (unspoken or unconscious agreements, in Sills, 1997).

Within organisational settings the business contract will be fully or partly determined by the organisation. In this context the assessor and the therapist always have to consider what is possible in that particular setting. Some of the examples of this will be explored below.

REFLECTIVE PRACTICE AND DOUBLE-LOOP LEARNING

Schön (1983) developed his concepts about reflective practice by investigating the practice of different professionals. He compared the multifaceted skills of a therapist with that of an artist:

> *[The psychotherapist] gives an artistic performance . . . in his selective management of large amounts of information, his ability to spin out long lines of invention and inference, and his capacity to hold several ways of looking at things at once without disrupting the flow of inquiry.*
> (1983, p130)

These skills are as essential in assessment as they are in clinical practice. The double-loop learning invites the practitioner to consider underlying assumptions behind their expressed goals and strategies. Self-awareness is an essential part of this process, but it is not sufficient in itself.

Etherington (2004) writes about the concept of reflexivity in research, and this is applicable to assessments. Reflexivity is a dynamic process, a reflection on the interaction between the therapist, the client and the context. The assessor needs to use their reflexivity to assess the needs of the client and whether the service can meet them, and to reflect on their own life, assessment skills and the organisation's norms and policies. This type of reflection forms double-loop learning within an assessment process.

Case study 4.2

Joan, an assessor within a counselling service, is meeting a new client. The client is Zack, a man in his late forties. He has been referred to counselling by his community psychiatric nurse (CPN), whom he sees regularly. Zack has had difficulties since his teens; he had several psychotic breakdowns in his twenties and was hospitalised, and he is currently on antipsychotic medication. He has been unemployed for a number of years, lives on his own and has no close friends or family. He struggles to make relationships, and feels very low and becomes anxious when he meets new people. Although he doesn't drink, Zack uses cannabis daily in order to relax – he doesn't see this as a problem. He has tried counselling before but it has never worked for him. However, he gets on well with his CPN who thinks counselling might help. He is not sure what he might gain from it, but feels that it would be good to talk to someone.

He speaks slowly, without making eye contact with Joan. She experiences a profound feeling of sadness while listening to Zack. She feels touched by his loneliness and isolation and wants to help. She has experience of working in a psychiatric hospital and Zack reminds her of some her patients. She wishes, fleetingly, that she could take him on.

Later on in supervision she talks about the assessment. Her belief is that Zack could indeed benefit from counselling, and she is wondering whether to refer him to someone. However, the practitioners who work within the service don't have the experience of severe mental health problems, and the service has a policy of not taking on clients diagnosed with a psychotic disorder.

REFLECTION POINT

- What do you think happened in the interaction between Joan and Zack?
- What does Joan need to learn about herself as an assessor?
- Is the organisational policy appropriate in this instance? Or does it need to change?

COMMENT

These are the types of questions that regularly emerge in the assessment process in organisations. Assessors need to consider the impact of their relationship with the client and the interface with the organisation. Double-loop learning is a learning opportunity for both the practitioner and the organisation to continue to develop their ability to meet the clients.

ETHICAL ISSUES

Themes of reflexivity and double-loop learning are also important in considering the ethical issues in organisational assessment.

The principles of fidelity, autonomy, beneficence, non-maleficence, justice and self-respect are as valid in organisational assessments as they are within private practice. In addition, organisations will usually have a set of ethical codes as well as policies and procedures to ensure good practice. It is the role of the assessor to know and understand those principles and deal with any dilemmas that might arise.

ACTIVITY 4.2

Consider the following scenario. The psychotherapy/counselling contract at the Metanoia Counselling and Psychotherapy Service (MCPS) states some limitations to confidentiality, and clients are asked to give their GP's contact details for emergencies. A client comes for an assessment but states that she wants a guarantee that her GP will not be contacted. She says that this is her reason for not seeking help within the NHS. She has not disclosed any history of violence to self or others, seems to be functioning well and is not on any medication.

- What would be options for you as an assessor in this case?
- Write up the options you have come up with and consider them in terms of the BACP ethical principles.
- Would you have dealt with this differently in private practice?

OVERVIEW OF ORGANISATIONS OFFERING PSYCHOLOGICAL THERAPIES

Organisations offering counselling and psychotherapy are varied in size, internal structure and assessment aims. In reviewing the types of assessment organisations we can divide the agencies broadly into statutory health services, educational establishments and voluntary agencies.

Statutory sector

Within the statutory sector the main access to counselling and psychotherapy is via primary care in the NHS and the stepped model of care (see Figure 4.1). Clinical guidelines are developed on the basis of research evidence and inform the national policy on the provision of services.

Figure 4.2 illustrates how the stepped care model is used within an IAPT (Improving Access to Psychological Therapies) service to assess clients for psychological treatments and refer them within the service (Prochaska and DiClemente, 1992).

Initial referral to the service is followed up by a 'triage assessment' by a mental health worker. Triage assessment is highly structured and questionnaire-based, and it provides uniformity in assessment and gives access to different psychological therapies, from psycho-educational interventions, counselling and groups to cognitive behavioural therapies. Triage assessment is often done by telephone. This initial basic assessment is followed by a more in-depth assessment by practitioners within different streams.

Step	Who	Condition	Intervention
Step 5	In-patient care, crisis teams	Risk to life, severe self-neglect	Medication, combined treatments, ECT
Step 4	Mental health specialists including crisis teams	Treatment-resistant, recurrent, atypical and psychotic depression, and those at significant risk	Medication, complex psychological interventions, combined treatments
Step 3	Primary care team, primary care mental health worker	Moderate or severe depression	Medication, psychological interventions, social support
Step 2	Primary care team, primary care mental health worker	Mild depression	Watchful waiting, guided self-help, computerised CBT, exercise, brief psychological interventions
Step 1	GP, practice nurse	Recognition	Assessment

Figure 4.1: The stepped care model (NICE, 2007)

Figure 4.2: Example of a stepped care model within IAPT service (CSIP [Care Services Improvement Partnership], 2008)

Pathway – Step up/down

Triage to steps 2, 2a and 3

Sep 2 – Ass and treatment at either 2a, 2b, 3

Step 2a – Ass at 2a (sideways step), 2b or 3

Step 2b – Ass at 2b (sideways step) or 3

Step 3 – Ass at step 2b

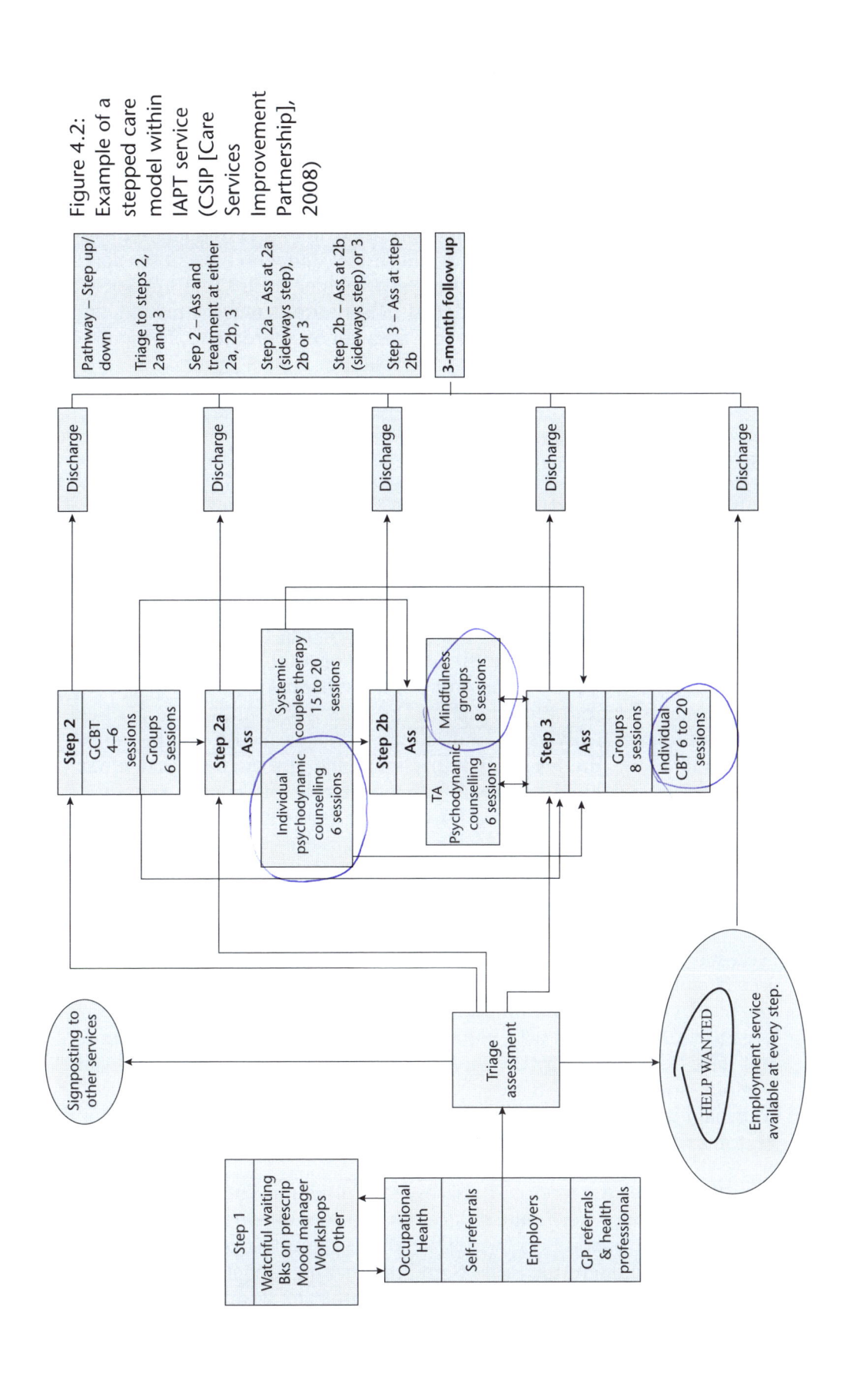

3-month follow up

This system is adapted to working with a large number of patients. The advantage is that clients receive an in-depth assessment only from the person who will be conducting therapy, and they therefore do not develop a relationship with the initial assessor, who will not end up working with them. The highly structured way of dealing with referrals ensures less delay in dealing with high referral numbers. A disadvantage is that a potentially complex process of assessment is conducted by staff who have little experience and do not provide therapy themselves, which means that some of the complexities and subtleties in clients' presentations may be missed, and clients may be referred to services that may not be appropriate. This potential limitation is addressed by the supervision of mental health workers by more experienced staff.

Educational institutions

Educational institutions that provide psychological therapies can be divided into higher education services and school counselling. In school counselling, teachers normally refer the children to the counsellors, who do their own assessment prior to conducting work with a child.

University counselling services usually offer brief or time-limited therapy. They are normally funded by the university and offer treatment to their own students only. Their client group is therefore more limited in age and educational background than that of the NHS. The counselling provided is free of charge. University counselling services vary in the theoretical orientations and the levels of staff experience and training. They may combine fully qualified, paid staff with students on placement. The role of the assessor in these organisations is to assess whether the service is appropriate for the client and make a referral to one of the practitioners.

Voluntary/non-statutory organisations

Non-statutory agencies and university counselling services have similarities in that counselling/psychotherapy provision is staffed either by students on placement or a combination of trainees and qualified staff. Some organisations also work with volunteers who have no professional training but have been trained by the service. This represents a minority of organisations, and they are usually specialised (e.g. some bereavement services). The majority of these agencies have at least some funding from the statutory sector, and some charge clients a low fee for their services.

Like the university services these organisations may offer a number of theoretical approaches. Some services offer groups or couples' counselling/psychotherapy in addition to individual sessions. Most offer time-limited treatments, although this varies from brief therapy models of six to twelve sessions to medium-term therapy of six months to a year; some offer more than a year of treatment. The role of the assessor in these organisations is usually matched to the specific organisation. The assessor decides whether the service can meet the needs of the client and must be aware of the learning needs and abilities of the practitioners.

ASSESSMENT METHODS

When deciding on assessment methods, organisations are faced with the challenges of resources and depth. The NHS, voluntary agencies and university services either do not charge for the service or charge low fees. The impact of dealing with limited resources and waiting lists puts additional pressure on the role of the assessor and may affect the resources allocated to the assessment process. Clinical assessment can be seen as a highly skilled and complex task requiring a range of clinical skills and experience, or, at the other end of the scale, a 'triage assessment' that can be done by novices.

Depending on the overall organisational strategies and resources, assessments can be conducted using different methods. Telephone assessment and face-to-face interviews are the two most common methods.

Telephone assessment

In deciding whether to offer telephone assessment, organisations need to consider a number of potential advantages and disadvantages.

An advantage of telephone assessment is the relative anonymity of this mode of communication, which can enable a client to be more open than they would be in face-to-face contact. The assessor who remains unseen is less likely to become an attachment figure, and this can help a client to make the transition to meeting their new therapist for the first time following the assessment.

From the perspective of organisational resources, telephone assessments are very efficient. They can be more structured than face-to-face sessions (like 'triage' assessments within the NHS) and take less time. They do not need a separate room for the assessment session and can therefore be more cost-effective for an organisation.

Some of the advantages of telephone assessments can also be seen as disadvantages. For example, the anonymity of a telephone assessment means it does not replicate the process of counselling in the same way that a face-to-face assessment interview does. The emphasis of a telephone assessment is potentially more on evaluation (identifying the needs of the client and evaluating whether the service can meet them) and less on preparing a client for the experience of counselling.

> ## ACTIVITY 4.3
>
> Imagine you are a client attending a telephone assessment. You have a letter with the name of the assessor. You are supposed to ring her at the appointed time.
>
> - What are your expectations?
> - What would you like to know from her?
>
> As you're speaking, you can hear the sound of her keyboard and vague computer noises. Occasionally you hear her take a sip of a drink.
>
> - What do you imagine about her surroundings?
> - How does it impact on you?

The assessor has a more narrow range of information to use in making the assessment and this can be particularly difficult when the assessors are inexperienced.

Another important consideration in deciding on the methods of assessment is the client's choice. Clients have different preferences, and some find the notion of talking to an unseen assessor by telephone difficult. At the Metanoia Institute we find that, given the choice, most clients prefer to have a face-to-face assessment session.

However, skilled telephone assessment can be an important resource within an organisation. In her book on telephone counselling Rosenfield (1997) cites research by McLennan that investigated the accuracy of telephone assessments and compared different counsellors in terms of their ability to conceptualise, their counselling skills and their responses to clients' needs. Their levels of performance were evaluated in relation to the accuracy with which they conceptualised the issues raised in the sessions. The study concluded that counsellors who had more experience in counselling and were generally more skilled were able to deal with more varied issues. These conclusions point to the telephone assessment method as suitable for more experienced assessors.

Rosenfield (1997) gives a list of essential categories of ability relevant in telephone assessments, and these are set out below. I have added reflection and suggestions from my experience at MCPS.

Welcoming the client
Welcoming the client to a telephone session needs to be carefully considered, bearing in mind that this form of appointment is not usual in other health services. Clients may feel unsure of the format, of the limits of the

session and of confidentiality, and need a brief introduction to the process. It is also important that the assessor introduces himself/herself and clarifies his/her role in both the organisation and the actual assessment.

Listening and responding skills
In my experience, listening and responding skills in this setting need to be overt. Assessors need to bear in mind that the client cannot see them or gauge the non-verbal signals.

Recognising and responding to feelings
This area is as important as in the face-to-face assessment. Listening out for changes in the tone of voice, pauses and background sounds can facilitate this process.

Working with transference and fantasy
Transference is defined by Holmes and Lindley (1998, p126) as: *the ways in which the feelings, wishes, and actions of the patient in relation to the therapist may be unconsciously influenced, coloured, and distorted by earlier childhood experiences, especially those with parents.* The general, 'fleeting transference' where prior hopes, expectations, assumptions, and fantasies impinge on interactions with doctors, therapists and other helpers without being necessarily encouraged or focused upon, are present in the telephone assessment as well as any other encounter. The assessor needs to bear in mind how this process may impact on the assessment.

Timekeeping
Clients can sometimes experience a telephone session as less formal than a face-to-face appointment. We are more used to using the telephone for social contact, particularly when talking about personal issues. In our experience at MCPS, maintaining the time boundaries of the assessment is essential. This emphasises the formality of the appointment and reflects the treatment. Time boundaries offer containment to the client in much the same way as they do in counselling. The impact of boundaries can often bring up personal issues relevant to the assessment process. For example, a client who needs to rearrange the assessment several times because of difficulties in managing commitments in their life presents the assessor with information relevant to the referral process.

Counsellor's personal and social skills
Personal and social skills are as important in the telephone appointment as in the face-to-face environment. The assessor's warmth and ability to relate will facilitate the process of the session in a way similar to the impact of these qualities on the process of counselling (Beutler et al., 1994; Beutler et al., 2004).

ACTIVITY 4.4

Put yourself in the role of an assessor with a booked telephone assessment interview. The appointment has been booked by letter and you have the client's personal details and his CORE questionnaire. The client's name is John Choudhury, he is 35 and unmarried. His CORE scores are all above the clinical cut-off.

- Make a note of things you would say to introduce yourself, the organisation and the assessment session.
- What are your aims in choosing to introduce it in this way?
- What might be the pitfalls?
- Given the information you have, what image do you have about the client?
- Given the information the client has about you – your name and title – what image do you think he might have of you?
- When you start to speak, what background noise will he hear from you?

During the assessment, the client talks about the recent break-up of a relationship. You hear a sigh, then silence; eventually his voice comes back, but sounds hesitant.

- What might have happened? How would you reflect on the emotion?

You are coming to the end of the session. You have given the client a five-minute warning and summarised the main points. He suddenly says: 'By the way, it probably isn't important for this, but I was molested as a child.'

- How might you address this, while maintaining the time boundaries?

In addition to Rosenfield's (1997) categories it is important to consider the context of the telephone assessment. How do clients book appointments? Does information gathering need to precede it? For example, you may need to have some personal and demographic information about the client in advance in order to save time in the assessment. You may consider sending out a standard questionnaire such as CORE Outcome Measure (CORE Information Management Systems) (see www.coreims.co.uk), which enables clients to give you more information about their experiences and difficulties prior to the interview.

The context has the potential to formalise the telephone assessment for both the assessor and the client. Completing information prior to the interview may help the client to prepare for the session and increase the likelihood of attendance (Mace, 1995a).

Obtaining information in advance can also help the assessor make the process faster as well as helping them begin to engage with a client.

COMMENT

When we don't have visual cues in contact with others we tend to rely more on other aspects of communication. We use their names, voices and how they communicate with us to imagine how people might be. Background noises become more noticeable in the silences.

Face-to-face assessments

As with telephone assessments, face-to-face assessment interviews within an organisational context have advantages and disadvantages.

Face-to-face assessments have the advantages of a more personal contact with clients and more opportunity for developing a relationship between the assessor and the client, and thus are more similar to the traditional counselling process. However, these can be seen as disadvantages too. Within an organisational structure, a practitioner who offers the initial assessment is not usually the person who offers counselling. Developing a therapeutic relationship with an assessor can lead to reluctance to engage with a counsellor who in some cases might be less experienced than the assessor. Tantum (1995) suggests that the close rapport between the assessor and the client may reduce satisfaction about a referral to another therapist and increase the likelihood of drop-out from treatment. A comparable problem may emerge if the assessment and treatment are in different theoretical modalities.

Another disadvantage is that face-to-face assessments require more organisational resources in terms of both staff and premises. The next chapter will offer a detailed analysis of the skills needed to conduct organisational assessments.

CHAPTER SUMMARY

This chapter highlights a number of similarities between private practice and organisations in the assessment skills and processes that are used.

- Concepts of transference and contracts are relevant to both. Ethical issues and consideration of the principles of reflective practice are important frameworks in organisations as well as the private practice.
- The organisational context impacts upon how the client experiences the assessment and the assessor. Issues of culture and difference, in their broadest sense, play a part in this process and need to be a part of the assessment. Reflective practice in organisations involves learning for both the assessor and the organisation, and good practice requires regular reviews of policies and procedures.

- Different organisations offer outpatient counselling and psychotherapy within statutory, voluntary and educational settings. Their resources vary a great deal, and they offer a varied range and scope of services. Assessment needs to balance clients' needs with the available service provision and resources.
- Telephone and face-to-face appointments can be used in organising initial assessments within organisations. For both, the advantages and disadvantages, as well as organisational resources and structure, need to be considered.
- The experience and skill of an assessor are important in enhancing the quality of telephone assessments, and questions about the assessor training and supervision are a vital consideration for organisations.

SUGGESTED FURTHER READING

Rosenfield, M (1997) *Counselling by telephone.* London: Sage.

This book explores the details of doing telephone assessments.

Sills, C (1997) *Contracts and contract making.* London: Sage.

This book gives an overview of different types of contracts with clients and reflects on their advantages and disadvantages.

CHAPTER 5

Conducting an assessment

> **CORE KNOWLEDGE**
>
> In this chapter we will learn how to assess clients within an organisational setting. In particular we will:
>
> - revisit some of the definitions of assessment and how they impact the assessment practice within an organisation;
> - learn the principles of structuring the interview;
> - address the issues of diagnosis in assessment by using clinical and relational diagnosis;
> - reflect on the client's narrative and how it can inform the diagnostic process;
> - learn about the principles, advantages and disadvantages of a formal clinical diagnosis (DSM IV-TR) in assessment;
> - look at principles and practice surrounding risk assessment.

INTRODUCTION

This chapter draws on the experience of conducting assessments within the Metanoia Counselling and Psychotherapy Service (MCPS) in combination with the wider professional literature about definitions, formats and content of assessment.

We introduce issues relating to diagnosis, including formal clinical diagnosis and risk assessment, and a broader therapeutic formulation using reflection on the client's narrative and assessment of motivation and readiness for change.

The assessment format at the MCPS has been gradually developed by me – as the head of the service – and the assessors working for MCPS. The components of assessment, skills and procedures that I present here have been identified during the collaborative action research project referred to in the introduction at the start of this book.

WHAT IS ASSESSMENT?

A number of authors have written about preliminary assessment in counselling and psychotherapy – some generically, some more specifically and in relation to a theoretical orientation. The following definitions of assessment are generic and can be used in organisations practising within different theoretical frameworks.

> **KEY CONCEPTS** Preliminary assessments
>
> In writing about the preliminary assessment, Ruddell (2009) quotes Malan (1979), who defines the assessment as a means of finding out what the problem is, how it developed and what should be done to resolve it. Malan recognises that different formulations within the assessment process are linked to different theories of mind within the counselling approaches and stresses the importance of trans-cultural issues.
>
> McMahon (2009) gives basic principles of taking a client's history within the preliminary assessment and offers administrative templates to help a beginner counsellor. She sees the key components as presenting problems, occupational and educational background, relationships and family history, medical history, previous counselling and outcomes, issues of ethnicity, sexuality and disability and any related problems. She recognises the use of questionnaires as an option.
>
> Tantum (1995) cites Wolberg (1977) in reflecting on the primary goals of a psychotherapeutic interview.
>
> - **Establishing a rapport with a patient** A therapist's skills involve the ability to attend to the client, empathy and acceptance. This rapport is more quickly established if the therapist and the client share similar values (Kantrowitz et al., 1990, cited in Tantum, 1995). However, not all the research supports this view, and some studies show that the similarity between the values of therapist and client has a different impact in short- and long-term therapy. At MCPS we have found that it is more relevant to assess how important the shared values might be to the client, rather than assuming that similarity will help. For example, a client who is struggling with the experience of oppression about being gay may prefer to have a therapist who shares his values. However, automatically referring an Asian client to an Asian therapist may go against the client's wishes and be counterproductive.

- **Obtaining patient information** This is essential in order to develop clinical diagnosis and diagnose potential psychosis and physical treatments.
- **Assessing clients' strengths as well as weaknesses** It is important for an assessor to recognise how clients may have approached solving their difficulties prior to coming to therapy and where they became stuck. For example, a client may have started off by reading books on bereavement, but became stuck in their loss because they haven't talked about their feelings to their friends and family.
- **Determining the cause and the beginning of presenting problems** For example, a client may become depressed following an external stressor, such as being made redundant. This may or may not have resonances with their past history.
- **Evaluating** the dynamics of the relationships in the client's life This is equally as important as the dynamics of the relationship with the assessor. An example is a client who experiences their work colleagues as being unjustly critical and who has also made several assessment appointments and arrived late.

The views of all the authors referred to are similar in that they recognise that the assessor has a role in forming a relationship with a client, taking the patient information and making sense of it in order to establish the best way forward. In the following sections, we will focus on specific assessment skills needed to fulfil those tasks.

STRUCTURING THE INTERVIEW

The question of how to structure the interview emerged as the first area assessors needed to learn about during their study at MCPS. It is particularly important in settings where the assessor has a single session in which to make a decision about whether to take the client into the service and, if so, to decide who to refer them to. The structure of the assessment session in this context is quite different from a traditional counselling/psychotherapy session, and the assessor usually has a predesigned format to help them.

In structuring the interview, Denford (1995) draws on Malan (1979) and suggests the basic aims of:

- gaining sufficient factual information to make a diagnosis;
- having enough information to allow the formulation of core issues in relation to the client's life experiences and development;

- using some therapeutic interventions that will give some idea of how the patient will respond to psychotherapy.

The assessment format used at MCPS (see Appendix 1) contains two sections: one relating to the client's demographic information and the CORE questionnaire completed prior to the assessment; and the second relating to structuring the interview.

The format relating to structuring the interview contains the following sections.

- *Presenting issues and current circumstances* Clients are asked about what brought them into therapy at this stage in their life in order to determine their motivation and hear the client's narrative of their presenting problems. In addition to this, assessors enquire into the client's current circumstances, such as whether they are in work (and whether they are experiencing any difficulties there) and whether they have close and/or supportive relationships. This gives information about the client's current level of functioning and supportive social networks that can sustain them through therapy.
- *Personal history* Clients are asked about their childhood and family history, as well as general developmental history, in order to gain insight into main relationship patterns and areas of developmental difficulty, such as attachment patterns and the history of trauma.
- *Therapeutic history* Clients have sometimes used a range of services. Insight into how they have used them and what they have found helpful and unhelpful helps the assessor think about how they might relate to the next counsellor and make decisions about who to refer them to.
- *Aims for the sessions* In this part of the interview clients are asked about their aims and hopes for the treatment. As well as clarifying what the client wants, this also gives the assessor an opportunity to offer some tentative formulations to the client. The assessor can reflect on the client's engagement with these formulations when making a referral.
- *Medication/health issues* This area includes information-gathering about substance use and about potential medical conditions that may impact the client.

REFLECTION POINT

- How would you structure the information you need to gain within an assessment session and what would you draw on?
- Are there any aspects of the suggested format that you think would not be useful or appropriate for your service?

Case study 5.1

Nell has come for therapy because she feels lonely and unconfident. Her relationships in the past have not been satisfactory. Her partners have been aggressive and often unfaithful. She despairs of ever having a good relationship. Nell sometimes meets men on the internet, but feels very ashamed of it. She is 43 and lives with her adult daughter. They are not close. She doesn't have close friends and has no contact with her family. Nell works in an office, but doesn't socialise with her colleagues.

Personal history
Nell was a middle child. Her parents split up when she was three and she had no contact with her father after that. Nobody was allowed to talk about him after he left. Nell found him when she was an adult; they met once, but has had no contact since then. Nell remembers her mother as angry and scary. There was a lot of fighting between her and her siblings. She did OK in school. She left home when she was 17 to live with her first boyfriend.

Therapeutic history
Nell saw a counsellor once for a couple of sessions. He didn't say much and she left. She said she didn't know what to say to him any more and couldn't see the point of continuing. She wanted someone who 'would talk back'.

Aims for the sessions
Nell wanted to see a counsellor to talk about her relationships with men. The counsellor said: 'I can see that this really matters to you. It seems that you might have felt lonely and unimportant to people for a long time.' Nell looked thoughtful. 'I never really felt loved by anyone. I kept hoping that one day it would happen for me, but it never did . . . I would like to look at that, what I do.'

Health issues
Nell has no current medical issues and is not on medication. She recognises that she often drinks too much in the evenings, when she is alone 'but it is not a problem, I can go without it'. The assessor asks her to estimate how much she might drink on average. 'A couple of glasses, two or three, maybe a bit more at the weekend.'

ACTIVITY 5.1

Reflect on the answers Nell has given and make a note of your responses.

- How would you make sense of the information she has given you? Use your theoretical orientation to formulate the core theme.
- Do you think she would be able to use counselling to address her difficulties? What might be stumbling blocks?

continued overleaf

> - What type of counsellor would you recommend for her, in view of her presenting issues and history?
>
> Now identify areas you would want to inquire into when assessing a client.
>
> - Are there any additional areas that would fit more with your orientation or the aims of your organisation? Reflect on your rationale for each of them.
> - Does this fit the needs of your organisation?
> - How much detail do you think you'll need for each area?

ASSESSING MOTIVATION AND STAGES OF CHANGE

The organisational enquiry within MCPS identified the assessment of the client's motivation as one of the essential skills assessors needed.

The transtheoretical approach offered by Prochaska and DiClemente (1992) is a model for identifying processes, levels and stages of change in psychotherapy. The processes of change relate to activities people use in order to change their thinking, feeling or behaviours relating to the problem. Prochaska (1984, cited in Prochaska and DiClemente, 1992) has identified ten processes of change people use both inside and outside the therapeutic environment: consciousness raising; self-liberation; social liberation; counter-conditioning; stimulus control; self-re-evaluation; environmental re-evaluation; contingency management; dramatic relief; and helping relationships.

Change involves the following stages.

- *Precontemplation* This is the time when people are least open to using the processes of change, and although they may be unmotivated to use therapy they may find themselves seeking counselling due to a life event or crisis; for example, a client may come to the assessment following the break-up of a relationship. The client may be in crisis, but has not necessarily committed to the level of reflection contained within the counselling process (Elton Wilson, 1996).
- *Contemplation stage* This is the time when clients are most open to using processes of change such as observations, confrontation and interpretation. They are most likely to use educational interventions, engage in self-evaluation and consider the impact of their behaviour on others. Exploratory interventions by the assessor can help to identify whether clients are able to use them. Use of self-help books and personal reflection prior to coming for an assessment can be indicators of this stage.

- *Preparation stage* At this stage clients are on the verge of taking action and need to set goals and plan accordingly. Examples would be clients who have had other therapy and have gained insight, but feel they need additional help to move forward.
- *Action stage* This arises from a sense of self-belief and responsibility for one's own actions. To reach this stage people need to have effective and cognitive foundation as well as be able to act. At the assessment stage, these are the clients who often need limited or short-term help to develop action and reflect on how to maintain the changes they have made.
- *Maintenance stage* This builds on each of the previous processes and involves an open assessment of conditions under which the person is likely to relapse.

In addition to the assessment of change processes and stages of change, Prochaska and DiClemente (1992) suggest that there are different levels of change that can be addressed by psychotherapy.

- *Symptoms/situational problems*, for example panic attacks or difficulties at work.
- *Maladaptive cognitions*, which are usually historical beliefs that limit functioning, for example, a client's belief that they will never have a close relationship because there is something wrong with them. This is based on the early attachments and subsequent relationship choices.
- *Current interpersonal conflicts*, for example, difficulties at work.
- *Family systems conflicts*, such as difficulties with a partner or a close member of the family.
- *Intrapersonal conflicts* – when a client is facing a difficult internal problem.

ACTIVITY 5.2

Analyse the following scenario and assess:

- the level and stages of change the client is presenting at;
- the processes of change he is currently using.

Steve works full time and lives with his partner. He is 26 years old. He has had a problem with alcohol since he was 16. He has stopped drinking for the last eight weeks. His partner is very understanding, although they don't talk about it. He doesn't have close friends. Steve never used to drink much during the week, but would binge-drink at weekends and end up having blackouts. He thinks he has a

continued overleaf

CONDUCTING AN ASSESSMENT

> low tolerance level and can't stop drinking when he starts. The last time this happened was at a family party. He ended up falling over and then drank all day the following day at work. He felt very scared about this and decided to stop and seek help. He realises he often feels unconfident and inferior to others.
>
> Steve's father had a history of alcoholism and died from an alcohol-related accident when Steve was 15. Steve's parents split up when he was ten and he had no contact with his father after that; he did not attend the funeral. Shortly after his father's death Steve started going out a lot and drinking with his friends. He remembers wanting to feel accepted by the group. He remembers being scared of the father as a child and finding him unpredictable and violent. He experienced his mother as supportive, but she was often away working. They never talked about his father after his death. He did OK in school, but didn't go into further education. This is his first long-term job and first long-term relationship. A year ago Steve attended AA (Alcoholics Anonymous) for a couple of months, but he didn't find it helpful. He would like to explore his relationship to alcohol and understand himself better. He would like to feel more confident.
>
> *Alcohol intake*: at weekends, at least ten glasses of vodka in a bar and then one bottle of vodka at home.
>
> *Smoking*: has increased, at least 15 per day.
>
> *Use of drugs*: 12 months ago was the last time he took cocaine and ecstasy.

COMMENT

We could assume that this client is in the stage of *precontemplation*. He is motivated by a crisis situation, but this is no evidence that he will be able to use counselling. He has stopped using alcohol relatively recently and may relapse when he is under stress. However, this does not mean that he would not be accepted for counselling at all. An exploratory agreement may give him an opportunity to find out whether he can use counselling to help him address his difficulties.

ROLE OF A NARRATIVE

An assessment session normally involves a client recounting a story of their life or creating a narrative. In psychotherapy in general, as well as in the assessment process, narratives play an important role.

McLeod (1997) writes about narratives in psychotherapy in the context of the importance that narratives and stories have had throughout human history in representing knowledge and resolving conflict. He suggests that narratives imply a relational world where there is a narrator and an audience. In the assessment session, the client is the narrator and the assessor is the audience.

Denford (1995) adds another element to the process of creating a narrative. He suggests that creating a narrative involves a complex cognitive process of organising the information and that this is impacted by the relationship with the assessor. He suggests that composing a life story in the context of an assessment presents a *central dynamic issue with large potential consequences for treatment* (Denford, 1995, p51).

COMMENT

The client in Case study 5.1 – Nell – has created a narrative of loneliness and disinterest, rejecting others in the assessment. This suggests a repeating theme in all relationships, including sexual relationships with men, which is the presenting issue. The question arises of how this theme might be repeated in the therapeutic relationship.

KEY CONCEPTS   Attachment

The concept of attachment, initially developed by Bowlby (1982), refers to the developmental process of seeking proximity to an identified attachment figure (normally a care giver) in situations of perceived distress or alarm. Mary Ainsworth developed her attachment theories between 1963 and 1978 (cited in Wallin, 2007) and discovered differences in attachment styles related to the behaviour of the care givers. This discovery led to the classification of attachment styles and the understanding of the differences between secure attachment and insecure attachment styles (Wallin, 2007).

COMMENT

Nell could be said to have an insecure attachment style. She does not seem to form secure attachments and her personal history may be pointing to the early roots of this pattern.

Clients' attachment patterns and styles are an important area and the assessor would have to reflect upon what type of therapist and what sort of interaction would provide a good enough balance of contact to enable Nell to feel sufficiently heard to explore these painful issues, while not attempting to meet them fully in the therapeutic context. This is where the importance of the therapist's 'person' and their attachment pattern, as well as their theoretical orientation, come into focus. Mohr et al. (2005) investigated the attachment patterns of clients and counsellors as predictors of outcomes and found that countertransference was highest (and the least helpful to the outcome) when the client had a preoccupied attachment pattern (and looked for reassurance and contact when distressed) and the counsellor had a fearful or dismissing attachment pattern (and avoided contact when distressed). An example might be the situation where a therapist with a dismissing attachment pattern goes on holiday, their client becomes distressed and the therapist meets the distress by being dismissive ('I've only been away for a week!').

The assessor has an active role in the assessment session and therefore impacts on the story the client tells about their life. Assessors ask questions to balance the client's narrative with the information they need for the assessment, and in this way take part in shaping it. Who the assessor is is important in this process.

REFLECTION POINT

- When someone asks me why I moved to the UK, I talk about aspects of my experience and create a story that depends on our relationship, what I'm feeling at the time and the context. Each story is true, but it may focus on professional issues, the emotional experience or relationships. Have you experienced this in everyday life?

ACTIVITY 5.3

Imagine telling the story of your life, to a friend, a colleague or at a job interview.

- What are the similarities? And differences?

The client's narrative may also be influenced by telling a story in combination with formal questionnaires. Tantum (1995) wrote about the experience of combining the use of questionnaires and a narrative at the Coventry Psychotherapy Service. Questionnaires were used to obtain historical data, and during the interview this was organised into a narrative. This was an approach also used at MCPS.

The style of the narrative within the assessment is often as important as the content and has diagnostic implications. For example, discontinuities in the narrative might point to psychosis, organic states or post-traumatic stress. Even when that is not the case, they give information about the style of relationships a client has and their thinking (Tantum, 1995).

A CLIENT'S NARRATIVE IN THE ASSESSMENT SESSION

In our collaborative study at MCPS, the assessors discussed the role of the client's narrative in the assessment session.

> *Assessor 1*: So, what is assessment? Is it a story telling?
> *Assessor 2*: I think the story's quite important, and the way the client tells it, and sometimes I look at my notes and think 'Oh that's quite a disorganised story' or 'That's a very clear story', or, you know, the narrative.
> *Supervisor*: So if the story was disjointed and didn't quite add up, and neither did the client in the assessment . . .?
> *Assessor 2*: I made a note, in the assessment notes, just under the comments that the client didn't maintain eye contact, and I did mention a few things when I referred her.
> *Supervisor*: So there's something potentially quite chaotic and fragmented about her, the way she comes across? You know how she tells the story and how she is in a relationship. So that's a really good example of how you use the story, as well as your experience of the client, to make an assessment.

During further discussion assessors also began to realise that clients often disclosed experiences of abuse in response to an apparently unrelated question, or towards the end of an assessment, and this impacted on their interest in the narrative.

> *Assessor 2*: So I'm sort of more interested in the narrative, in the story and in thinking about the story – not just hearing what the story is. But it is also important to think about how it's told and the purpose of it because I think at one point I said to you I was worried that all I was doing in the assessments was listening to stories. And it was very interesting that you said that there's a lot in the story as well. And I think that sort of sunk in somehow, so I'm beginning to see the importance of the storytelling bit with my clients.

ACTIVITY 5.4

Think of the narrative a client has presented in an assessment and reflect on the following.

- Organisation of the narrative: does it seem fragmented or continuous?
- Clarity: which elements seem clear? What is your experience of the whole story?
- Relationships in the narrative: what is the role the client sees themselves in, in relation to others?
- Relationship with you: how do you experience this client? Reflect on the feelings, images and the impact of the client's story? How do you think the client experiences you?
- What is the cultural context of the client's narrative? How does this interact with your cultural context? What is the context of your organisation?
- Make a formulation on the basis of this reflection.

CONDUCTING AN ASSESSMENT: CLINICAL DIAGNOSIS

The issue of using formal clinical diagnosis (such as DSM) in assessment for psychotherapy and counselling is complex. What is diagnosis (and what is it not)? How can it be useful (and what might be the damaging aspects of it)?

In psychotherapy literature there are a number of warnings about the uses of formal diagnosis. In contrast, the statutory services routinely use formal diagnosis to identify appropriate treatments for clients. Diagnostic methods such as DSM-IV are also commonly taught in psychotherapy training, alongside the theoretical formulations. Approaches such as cognitive behavioural therapy have developed strategies and treatments specific to different diagnostic categories.

Within the statutory services, formal diagnosis offers a common language that enables medical professionals, psychologists and psychotherapists to communicate and to co-ordinate treatment for clients and assess risk. Refusal to use formal diagnosis in such settings could potentially curtail clients' access to services. However, there are a number of potential disadvantages to psychiatric diagnosis: for example, it can be disrespectful and labelling for a client and it may not capture the complexity and individuality of their presenting circumstances and experience.

In writing about assessment for inpatient treatment, Elfant (1985) suggests the importance of the difference between assessment and diagnosis. The assessment needs to be consistent with the psychological principles of personal responsibility, respect for the private experience of the patient, and efforts to examine meaning and communication. If that is not the case, we could be in danger of overemphasising DSM categories at the expense of interpersonal and psychological factors. Diagnosis in this context needs to be an 'operational diagnosis' (Cummings and VandenBos, 1979), focusing on the effect of the patient's maladaptive patterns on the person's life.

Beutler (1989) also strongly suggests that psychiatric diagnoses are of little value in predicting the outcomes of psychotherapy because the dimensions that underlie psychiatric diagnoses appear to be different from the principles of psychotherapy. A different approach to diagnosis appears in the use of theoretical formulations in the assessment.

> **KEY CONCEPTS** Exploring client relationships
>
> Hinshelwood (1995) writes about the importance of exploring three areas of clients' relationships in the assessment session.
>
> - Current life situation – for example, relationships with partners and children, work relationships and friendships.
> - Historical relationships – normally relationships with primary carers and siblings.
> - Relationship with the assessor – this relates to how the client presents in the session, assessor's countertransference but also how the referral arrives and any contact there may be prior to the session.

Awareness of these three areas provides the assessor with what Hinshelwood refers to as the *baseline hypothesis* of the common theme and the core of the pain the client is attempting to deal with. He suggests that in the assessment for psychodynamic psychotherapy it is important that the assessor makes the interpretation. His suggestion is that this does not serve to deepen the relationship with the assessor (which would not be advisable) but confronts the client with the painful theme in their life and enables the client to leave the assessor.

In relation to this Denman writes:

> *Ideally, the formulation acts as a lens which can focus the many details of the case into a coherent vision.*
>
> (1995, p180)

Da Rocha Barros (2002), in his reflection on the first appointment and subsequent sessions with his patient, shows how the issues that presented themselves in the early relationship with the psychoanalyst became more apparent in the subsequent sessions. Identifying those major themes can help the assessor identify the best way forward in referring the client.

Related to the focal theme and the relationship history is the concept of attachment (Bowlby, 1982), which we referred to in the previous section. Eagle (2006) discusses the role of attachment theory in psychotherapy and cites a study by McBride et al. (2006) that has made a major contribution to this issue by demonstrating, in a randomised clinical control trial, that attachment theory can usefully inform clinical thinking by encouraging therapists to take the patient's attachment pattern into account when selecting a treatment approach.

This leaves us with the question of whether formal diagnosis and DSM categories can be used in the reflective assessment process. During the collaborative enquiry at MCPS, different assessors used different theoretical orientations and did not share the same therapeutic language. In order to communicate with one another and with me as the supervisor, they used DSM categories (Axes I–V) to help them to develop a lens to create a baseline hypothesis.

The following is an example of using countertransference to create a formulation. The client in this case withheld an important piece of information from the assessor that became apparent only at the end of the session. The assessor is reflecting on her experience of the client.

Assessor 3: I found the client personally uncomfortable.
Supervisor: Well, how do you use your countertransference? What was *your* discomfort?
Assessor 3: What was it about him that made me uncomfortable? His grandiosity. I thought he was playing; I thought he was being manipulative and he was making me feel that he was covering something up, not being straight.
Supervisor: So your countertransference was correct.
Assessor 3: So I guess what I'm learning is that countertransference is actually a good clue in assessments; it's not just subjectivity.
Supervisor: It's your data. It is subjective and it is data concerning what happens between you. But it sounds like in this case you have a really good example of how that was accurate. Because he was covering up, no – there are things that he didn't tell you and I'm sure there are more things that he didn't tell you.

COMMENT

In this example the assessor is learning to reflect on the relationship with the client in the room and the importance of using intuition in the assessment as a way to open up and explore areas clients may not disclose immediately, but also to recognise the limits of intuition. In doing this she differentiates between the assessment content (and what the client said) and the client's behaviour, presentation and relationship with the assessor. Sometimes the relevant themes do not emerge in the assessment session itself, but emerge prior to it, during the ending process or after the session. For example, a client who has disclosed a history of abuse might have difficulties in ending the assessment session.

> *Assessor 2*: I'm interested in how her difficulties came more at the boundary edge than in the actual assessment.
> *Assessor 1*: Yes, I felt that, relationally, she was really opening up gradually because it was quite a difficult assessment in terms of, you know, her whole history of abuse. I felt really challenged by it. But what was actually more challenging in a way was the boundary issue and finishing it.

COMMENT

Within this process of reflecting on their subjective experiences assessors also began to discuss the use of DSM-IV criteria in more detail and depth. Examples of clients presenting problems led to a discussion about Axes I, IV and V. The information about the historical relationships and the relationship between the client, the assessor and the process of the assessment session led to a reflection on Axis II disorders and in some cases a detailed diagnosis of personality disorders and traits.

Case study 5.2

A client who has disclosed a long history of sexual and physical abuse in childhood is currently seeking therapy because she feels unable to care for her young child. She has a violent, alcoholic partner and a history of drug abuse. She frequently falls out with her friends and struggles with authority figures. She has been unable to sustain working for anything other than short periods of time. When she is distressed she sometimes cuts herself, but reassures the assessor that this is not frequent. The client is late for the assessment and angry when the assessor reflects on it, but seems to extend the session by adding more and more detail to her narrative. After the assessment she changes her mind several times about the days she will be available for psychotherapy. The assessor is tired and angry by the end of this process, and her countertransferential response is about a 'difficult client', where nothing is 'good enough'. She has experienced an invitation from the client

continued overleaf

to reject her. The baseline theme of being not good enough and being rejected is at the core of this client's experience and will form a major therapeutic theme in the subsequent psychotherapy. The need to be available and attentive while holding the boundaries will ultimately be important in the therapist's therapeutic stance. The assessment encounter therefore provides a significant lens on the client's experiences and has a predictive value.

Using DSM-IV diagnosis the assessor reflected on:

- Axis I – areas of post-traumatic stress and addictions;
- Axis II – area of personality disorders, particularly the borderline personality disorder traits;
- Axis III – the medical conditions;
- Axis IV – difficulties in her primary relationships;
- Axis V – the general assessment of functioning.

COMMENT

The psychiatric diagnosis could help the assessor to further clarify the severity of the issues the client presents with and help them not only to make the allocation but also think further of other services the client might need. The question arises about the involvement of the social services and the client's GP, with a potential referral to the community mental health team.

ACTIVITY 5.5

Think of a recent assessment you conducted. Identify:

- the client's presenting problem;
- the historical significant relationships in the client's life;
- the client's relationship with you in the session.

Hypothesise on the common themes in all these areas.

- How is this significant for the presenting issue the client has brought?

Now using the Axes of DSM-IV, assess the client further.

- On the basis of this assessment, do you think the client will benefit from counselling?
- Will the client need access to other services?

CONDUCTING AN ASSESSMENT: RISK ASSESSMENT

Assessment of risk is an important part of assessment for counselling, as well as an area of diagnosis.

Curwen (1997) writes about the importance of psychiatric diagnosis in assessment for counselling and focuses on risk assessment. He separates different areas of risk in relation to the client's overall mental functioning, risk to the therapist and risk of suicide.

Curwen refers to the diagnosis as a methodical way of gathering information in order to gain a better picture of the client, the extent of their symptoms and their involvement with other agencies. He stresses the importance of agency collaboration, particularly where there is an area of risk. The assessment of the client's mental state involves the client's behaviour, symptoms and the interpersonal dynamics at the time of the assessment. This is of particular importance in assessing risk.

KEY CONCEPTS Assessing risk

Curwen (1997) also suggests the importance of psychiatric, social and physical factors preceding suicide and provides several key areas for consideration when assessing risk.

- *Age and gender* Overall there is greater risk of suicide for men between 25 and 35, women in their late 50s and men over 60.
- *Symptoms* There is a greater risk if the client is depressed or uses substances such as alcohol and drugs.
- *Stress* There is a greater risk if the client is under a significant amount of stress.
- *Suicidal plan* Risk increases if there is a detailed plan of suicide, prior suicide attempts or a family history of suicide.
- *Physical illness* The risk increases if the client is suffering from a debilitating or chronic physical illness.
- *Support/interpersonal relationships* Risk increases if the client does not have supportive relationships and feels rejected or alienated.

The area of risk assessment requires a high degree of attention by the assessor and a willingness to address difficult issues with the client in the session. The structure Curwen (1997) suggests involves using the formal diagnosis as well as paying attention to the quality of contact with the assessor.

CONDUCTING AN ASSESSMENT

The assessors in our collaborative project reflected on the importance of risk assessment and relevance of the countertransferential experience in addition to the overt exploration of the suicidal content and thoughts. In the following passage, they focus on the experience of detachment.

> *Assessor 3*: And then all of a sudden I sat up and realised that this woman is talking about wanting to throw herself in front of the Tube. She doesn't know whether she's going to make it to next week, that kind of thing. And that she'd spoken to the GP and the GP hadn't picked up on it at all. At that point I just sent her back straight to the surgery and suggested that she see a different GP and that she stressed to that GP exactly how she's feeling. Because I was getting the feeling that she was kind of 'Oh shall I throw myself under this train or not?', a bit you know . . .
> *Supervisor*: She's that detached?
> *Assessor 3*: Yes. And with her distress signals, she wasn't showing people how distressed she was and I kind of felt I was in a place of second guessing it really.

COMMENT

This experience was followed by using the formal diagnosis to assess the risk. The assessor reflected on the client's history (which involved multiple suicide attempts), general functioning (such as long-standing depression), lack of employment or supportive relationships and her suicide plan (which was present but did not contain details of exact actions and timing). She recognised that the client was at risk and that accepting her for therapy would require involvement and collaboration with the client's GP. Her intuition and countertransferential experiences of detachment and shock served to alert her to the risk factors, which she could then follow up diagnostically.

Assessment in these circumstances offers a degree of containment to the client but also – where counselling is not appropriate or advisable – the possibility of creating a gateway to other services. Different organisations have sets of procedures about dealing with risk.

CHAPTER SUMMARY

- In this chapter we have introduced some of the principles and practices of conducting an assessment within an organisation. We have suggested the development of a formal template that assessors can use to structure the assessment and we have stressed the importance of the client's presenting issues, current functioning,

relationships and health, motivation, personal and counselling history, and aims for therapy.
- The question of a client's readiness for therapy was addressed by reflecting on motivation and stages of change using the transtheoretical model (Prochaska and DiClemente, 1992).
- The question of diagnosis in the assessment process invited reflection on developing a formal clinical diagnosis, formulating or understanding the focal theme in the presenting issues, and understanding the client's attachment pattern.
- A client's narrative was introduced as one of the key concepts in the assessment process giving insight into the central themes in a client's life and relationships, their aim for therapy, and their cognitive functioning, trauma and attachment patterns.
- Assessment of risk was addressed in relation to age, gender, health, personal history of behaviours related to harm to self and others, relationships and the quality of contact with the assessor, and the need for involvement by other agencies.

SUGGESTED FURTHER READING

American Psychiatric Association (1994) *DSM–IV–TR: Diagnostic and statistical manual of mental disorders*. Arlington, VA: American Psychiatric Press Inc.

This is an essential resource in developing a formal clinical diagnosis. A quick reference is also available.

Prochaska, J and DiClemente, C (1992) The transtheoretical approach, in Norcross, JC and Goldfried, MR (eds) *Handbook of psychotherapy integration*. New York: Basic Books, pp300–34.

This gives a detailed description of stages and levels of change.

Chapter 6

Assessment skills

> **CORE KNOWLEDGE**
>
> In this chapter we will:
>
> - learn about the assessment skills 'balancing containment and listening' and 'using probing' – both skills were identified by the collaborative action enquiry at MCPS;
> - consider the use of questionnaires in organisational assessment;
> - reflect on different assessment outcomes and options;
> - consider the use of different types of contracts with clients in relation to assessment outcomes;
> - reflect on the complexity of the assessor's role and the impact of assessments.

INTRODUCTION

This chapter presents some of the specific skills and strategies used in assessment. The skill of balancing containment and listening arises from the need to establish the relationship with the client, keep to the boundaries of the session and structure the interview. The skill of using probing comes from the need to assess risk and identify core themes in a single session. Both of these skills are particular to an organisational assessment where the assessor does not continue the therapeutic work with the client. The use of questionnaires will also be presented from this perspective.

The assessor in organisations has a particular role in deciding the assessment outcome with the client and referring them to the appropriate service. In this chapter we will look at factors and options that can support the assessor in this process.

Finally, the role of an assessor within an organisation contains particular complexities and stressors. We will reflect on these and suggest some ways forward.

BALANCE BETWEEN CONTAINMENT AND LISTENING

In order to conduct an assessment session and establish a relationship with a client it is important to balance the skills of containment and boundary setting with listening.

The containment of time boundaries in the assessment serves the same function as it does in the counselling session. As well as the practical reasons for keeping to the time, keeping to the time boundaries models the therapeutic process. It also communicates to clients that their presenting issues are manageable and containable.

The balance between containment and listening has another purpose too. In the words of one assessor:

> I've had a run of very distressed clients, one after the other, and I was actually really mindful of containing them and not allowing them to go to where they were wanting to go, and actually just putting my pen down and forgetting about the assessment – there was a real tension between containment and holding and being therapeutic, and still allowing there to be an assessment element, sort of getting enough information and appropriate information about the client, but also to somehow stop them going where they were wanting to go, sort of retraumatising them to some extent.

The assessor is referring to the process of deciding about the amount of personal disclosure that would be therapeutic and sufficient for the purposes of the assessment while maintaining the client's best interests and safety. The assessment session, during which an interested professional is enquiring about one's life, is an invitation to disclose details that can often be very personal and sometimes painful. This is usually helpful. A client can experience a sense of relief and begin to reflect on their difficulties. However, if a client has experienced a significant trauma, recounting the experience without an established ongoing therapeutic relationship can be retraumatising (Cozolino, 2002; Rothschild, 2000). In these cases it is important for the assessor to help to contain the amount of detail that a client might wish to disclose.

Containing the information and the amount of detail in the session also enables the assessor and the client to reflect on the differences between the assessment session and the ongoing therapeutic relationship, thus helping to limit the attachment process with the assessor.

ASSESSMENT SKILLS

> ### ACTIVITY 6.1
>
> Imagine conducting an assessment session with a client who is having difficulties with her husband. She tells you that she has difficulties in their sexual relationship and feels frightened during intercourse. This leads her to tell you that she was sexually abused as a child, and she starts to talk about this. While she is talking her gaze seems to become unfocused, she becomes pale and starts to look agitated. She speaks fast and is starting to give you a very detailed account of her experiences.
>
> Reflect on the following issues.
>
> - What signals might alert you that the client is becoming too distressed and potentially retraumatised?
> - What information do you need to have for the assessment?
> - What do you *not* need to know? Describe your rationale.
> - How would you notice if the client is telling more than would be useful for her?

COMMENT

The client's body language and the manner of speaking might indicate that she is re-experiencing a traumatic event. It is important to consider how you could reduce the chances of this happening. For example, you may not need to know any details about the traumatic event, but only the nature of the trauma, when it happened and how the client dealt with it at the time. These are not definitive guidelines. At all times it is important to bear in mind the safety of the client.

SPECIFIC ASSESSMENT SKILLS: PROBING

The collaborative inquiry at the MCPS identified another skill that needs to be balanced with listening and containment and is of particular relevance in the organisational assessment – the skill of probing.

Probing allows the assessor to follow up the lines of their enquiry and make sense of what the client is presenting. This skill often combines advanced empathy (Egan, 1985) and the use of intuition in asking clarifying questions:

> *The process of active listening aided by focused, detailed questioning as summarising ideas begin to form, is at the heart of the assessment process.*
>
> (Denford, 1995, p53)

> *Supervisor*: And I think you've done incredibly well with listening and probing, and being able to say: 'Look, I'm not following, I don't know what it is.'
> *Assessor 2*: Yes, I think that's what I've learnt now. That if I don't understand it's because there's something that I need to explore further, and that that's OK. Because I think in the past I would just assume that I hadn't 'got' it or . . .
> *Assessor 3*: That it's you . . .

An assessor has only a limited time with and experience of the client. This means that some of the difficult issues relevant to the assessment may only be hinted at by the client.

> ### Using probing to assess substance abuse
>
> *Assessor*: How much alcohol do you drink in a week?
> *Client*: Sometimes more, sometimes less. I'm not an alcoholic, you know.
> *Assessor*: OK, so it's not always the same.
> *Client*: No, this week I haven't had anything.
> *Assessor*: And when you drink more . . .?
> *Client*: Well, I went out last time and I don't know how I got home. I don't remember much. I'd had a hard day at work.
> *Assessor*: Does it mean that you might drink quite a lot when something is bothering you?
> Client: I haven't thought about it like that before, but you're quite right. I hate doing it.

COMMENT

This is an example of how probing by the assessor begins to establish a pattern and the way the client deals with stress. The client starts to develop insight and this opens up a potential area for therapeutic work.

Using probing to assess the risk of violence

Another area where probing has a role is in identifying areas of risk. This requires that the assessor pays attention to the client's narrative and identifies the missing or unclear areas that might be related to issues of risk.

In the following passage, the client talks about difficulties with his partner and the arguments they have. His partner tells him that he has problems with anger and she is threatening to leave him.

> *Assessor*: Do you think you have difficulties with anger?
> *Client*: I'm not sure, that's why I'm here.
> *Assessor*: How do you express anger?
> *Client*: I shout mainly, throw things . . . I've never hurt anyone seriously.
> *Assessor*: Have you ever hit anyone?
> *Client*: Not really, not seriously. I pushed her. I hate it when she talks back to me.

COMMENT

In this case the assessor's focus and probing help to start identifying violence in the relationship and open up an area for further exploration.

SPECIFIC ASSESSMENT SKILLS: USE OF QUESTIONNAIRES

Assessors working in organisations tend to use broad assessment formats as structure. This often includes the use of formal and/or standardised questionnaires. Sometimes services ask clients to provide contact and demographic information in order to accelerate the assessment process (see Appendix 1). Standardised clinical questionnaires focusing on clients' symptoms and functioning, e.g. CORE and Beck's Depression Inventory (Beck, 2006), can be used to facilitate the diagnosis and risk assessment during the assessment, as well as for the evaluation of counselling that may take place after the initial appointment.

In 1993, Mace (1995b) conducted a survey of psychotherapy departments in the NHS. Questionnaires were routinely used, but there was little co-ordination. Most sent questionnaires to all newly referred patients. The survey asked the respondents to list the benefits they brought. Mace (1995b) found that therapists and clients mostly agreed about the benefits, which included ease of fact-gathering, improvement in attendance and improvement in preparation.

As disadvantages, authors listed the potentially demanding or discouraging nature of questionnaires and confidentiality concerns. Patients listed confidentiality as a concern, too. They also had concerns about their own ability to understand the questionnaires and answer the questions. Sometimes they felt disturbed by the questions and feared prejudice and shame. In summary, Mace (1995b) asserts that questionnaires have the potential to assist assessors by providing information that is useful in the assessment, useful for diagnosis and valuable for audit or research.

At MCPS, all clients are asked to complete the personal details form (see Appendix 1), the CORE Outcome Measure and the Beck Depression Inventory.

Assessors use the questionnaires collaboratively. Clients complete them prior to the assessment but they are discussed in the assessment session as well. The collaborative approach to using formal measures helps the assessor and the client to deepen the assessment and address some of the issues that Mace (1995b) refers to as 'clients' concerns' – confidentiality, literacy, fear of judgement and prejudice, and the disturbance created by the questions. For example, assessors can explain to the client the confidentiality of the setting and who will see the questionnaires. They can also explain that counsellors can help if a client does not understand some questions. It is important to talk to the client about how the questionnaires are an essential component to better understanding what the client's problems are and giving the client a way to monitor their own progress in therapy.

The reflection undertaken during the enquiry at MCPS suggested a number of ways in which clients approached questionnaires. For example, we found that clients used the questionnaires as a way of communicating with the assessor and the organisation. How they approached that depended on their current state of mind, motivation and personal style. The assessors used the information given in the questionnaires as an additional area of communication by the client in the assessment process.

Based on this experience we have found it helpful to view the responses to the questionnaires in the context of assessment as subjective narrative realities rather than the objective 'truth'.

This is often particularly helpful in the area of risk assessment (see Chapter 5). For example, questionnaires, such as the CORE Outcome Measure (Barkham et al., 2001), ask direct questions about risk to self and others. This creates an opening and expectation that such issues will be discussed in the assessment.

The questionnaire is often helpful in asking questions on subjects that the client may not think relevant to bring up in the session but that impact on general well-being and functioning (such as sleeping patterns, mood and anxiety).

ASSESSMENT OUTCOMES – MAKING A DECISION

Having conducted the assessment session, the assessor is then faced with making a decision about whether or not to accept the client for therapy. In the best circumstances, assessment is a collaborative process, during which the assessor and the client can openly discuss the best way forward. The aim of the assessor is to refer a client to an appropriate service, so the assessment needs to have a predictive value (Mash and Hunsley, 1993). This is not easy and there are no certain guidelines to ensure the appropriate referral.

ASSESSMENT SKILLS

Previously discussed strategies need to be taken into consideration when making a decision about referring a client. The assessor needs to be able to say 'no' when the service cannot meet the needs of the client, even if the client is motivated and in need. Limitations of the service usually relate to the length of treatment (sessions are usually time limited, sometimes brief), staff experience (there are no specialised staff or there are only students with limited experience) and the setting (for example, there is no access to direct medical or psychiatric support).

In cases where the risk factors cannot be sufficiently contained within the service – as in cases of severe psychological and psychiatric disorders, or where medical intervention may be needed – it is in the best interests of the client to be referred to the mental health service in the area.

Cooper (2008) reviews a range of client and therapist factors related to their effectiveness. In making a decision about referral, consideration needs to be given to these factors as well as the choice of theoretical orientation.

Client factors

Motivation and involvement

In their review of therapist, client and relational variables relating to effectiveness, Orlinsky et al. (1994) have found that a client's motivation and active participation in therapy are probably the most important factors in determining the outcomes. Related factors include expectations of a successful outcome, realistic expectations about the process of therapy and beliefs about the origins of the client's difficulties and how the change will happen (Cooper, 2008).

Psychological functioning

There are different aspects to psychological functioning and its impact on the benefits of psychotherapy. Overall, there is a suggestion that clients with higher levels of psychological dysfunction, such as can be seen in personality disorders (DSM-IV), tend to do less well in psychotherapy (Cooper, 2008) and consideration needs to be made about what would be the most suitable approach.

Perfectionism

A number of studies show that a client's perfectionism impacts adversely on the effectiveness of psychotherapy and the development of the working alliance (Blatt et al., 1996).

Psychological mindedness

Psychological mindedness has been defined as a *personality characteristic that clinicians usually use to connote an ability both to see causal relationships, ideas, feelings, and behaviour, and to recognise them in the first place* (Baekeland and

Lundwall, cited in Valbak, 2004). Baekeland and Lundwall's review found that psychological-mindedness was related to good outcomes in 92.3 per cent of studies they reviewed. Valbak's (2004) review of empirical studies on suitability for psychodynamic psychotherapy also shows that the highest correlations with good outcomes were psychological mindedness, motivation for change and 'good object relations'. Additional investigations have found psychological mindedness to be positively related to remaining in therapy (Chappel et al., Kissin et al., Mozdzierz et al. and Nelson and Hoffman, all cited in Valbak, 1994; DuBrin and Zastowny, 1988).

Attachment style
This has also been shown to have an impact on the ability to stay in therapy (Meyer and Pilkonis, 2002; Mohr et al., 2005). Clients with more secure attachment styles and better social networks tend to do better in therapy.

Therapist factors

In his review of literature on the therapist factors Cooper (2008) concludes that although there is a high level of difference in effectiveness between different psychotherapists, therapists' personal traits seem to have less impact than the way they relate to their clients. There is some evidence that therapists' attachment styles impact on the relationship with their clients (Mohr et al., 2005), and those therapists with higher levels of well-being have better outcomes. Although individual therapist characteristics of age, gender and ethnicity are not factors in effectiveness as such (Lambert and Ogles, 2004; Luborsky et al., 1985; Norcross, 2002), clients' preference for therapists with particular beliefs or from a particular background are associated with positive outcomes (Cooper, 2008).

Therapeutic approach

The question about which approach would be best is linked to the question about the effectiveness of psychotherapy orientations. Roth and Fonagy (2005) have published a detailed review of empirically supported therapies for particular forms of psychological distress. In contrast to this there is research about the equivalence of effectiveness between different theoretical orientations, known as the 'common factors research' (Lambert and Ogles, 2004; Luborsky and Singer, 1975; Wampold, 2001).

Summarising this debate, Cooper (2008) suggests that it is important to transcend this polarity and to use Paul's question for reflection on referral: *What treatment, by whom, is most effective for this individual, with that specific problem, and under which circumstances?* (Paul, 1967, p111, cited in Cooper, 2008). The client and therapist characteristics described above may be more relevant in choosing the orientation and the style of therapy.

Treatment options

Bearing in mind that clients arrive at assessment at different stages of motivation and stages of change, it may be appropriate to have a number of referral stages and choices following an assessment session.

Elton Wilson (1996) suggests the following choices for client and assessor after an assessment interview. The client can be assessed as willing to engage (or ready for therapy) in crisis (distressed but not seeking psychological change, for example, in bereavement) or 'visiting' (testing psychological therapy – for example, a GP may have recommended therapy, but the client is unsure). According to Elton Wilson, the choice points could then include the following.

- Life without therapy or referral to a different type of service (e.g. psychiatric referral or a befriending scheme).
- A holding arrangement (one to three sessions), which is particularly appropriate for clients in crisis. This could be followed by a review and perhaps another assessment where appropriate.
- A mini-commitment (four to six regular weekly sessions). This may be appropriate where the client is 'visiting' or testing psychological therapy. Review or another assessment session could follow this trial period of therapy.
- Referral to ongoing therapy within the service. This would involve reflection on the best therapist and treatment for this client, at this time in their life.

Case study 6.1

Sarah is a 48-year-old white woman. She is neatly dressed, her clothes are colour-co-ordinated and she is softly spoken. She is very slim. She has arrived ten minutes prior to the session and has completed all the relevant information and questionnaires. She works as a teacher and lives on her own. She and her long-term partner of 14 years broke up six months ago. He is now in a relationship with another woman. She knows that his new girlfriend is younger than her and pregnant.

Most of their friends are mutual and she feels she has no one to talk to. She has never had very close friendships and doesn't see her brothers. She has been feeling very low and is struggling to get over her ex-partner; she feels rejected and angry. She spends evenings mostly on her own and cuts her arms and stomach. She feels better at the time, but very ashamed afterwards.

Sarah is also assessing her life in general, wondering how she ended up alone and without children.

She finds her job stressful, but is able to perform her role. She is not close to any of her colleagues and prefers to keep herself to herself. Most of them have families and children.

Sarah comes from a Catholic family and grew up with both parents and three brothers. She was the second youngest child. She was always a 'good girl' and never seemed to get into trouble at home or school. Her father was violent, and used to hit her brothers, although she was never hit. There were a lot of arguments at home and she felt desperate to leave. She didn't get on with her brothers, and used to spend a lot of time by herself. Sarah started to drink and cut herself as a teenager in order to feel more confident in social situations. She had her first boyfriend when she was 13 and left home to live with him when she was 17. They didn't stay together long; he left her for another girl. She didn't have other relationships until she met her last partner.

Sarah had counselling for her heavy drinking ten years ago and has managed to control it. She used a specialised service and had 12 sessions. She described her counsellor as friendly and liked it that he didn't seem to judge her or tell her what to do.

The client wants to get to a point where he can feel less unhappy with her life. She would like to understand her feelings better and let go of the past. Sarah's health is generally good. She uses alcohol every day, approximately half a bottle of wine in an evening and more at weekends. She is not worried about her drinking and doesn't want to focus on it in the sessions. She used to drink more in the past.

ACTIVITY 6.2

Using the information in the case study, reflect on the following.

- *Motivation and expectations of therapy* Sarah has had counselling before. Do you think she has realistic expectations of what it involves? Her alcohol intake is far higher than the healthy recommended amounts, but she does not want to focus on it in therapy. What do you think would be a possible impact of this?
- *Psychological functioning* What do you think is the level of Sarah's psychological functioning? It may be useful to use the DSM-IV to reflect on this. Does her self-harming necessitate involvement with other agencies? Do the staff in your organisation have sufficient experience to deal with self-harming?
- *Perfectionism* Do you think there is any evidence of perfectionism in Sarah's presentation? How do you think that might affect the therapeutic process?
- *Attachment style* Sarah has no close relationships, apart from her male partners. How would you assess her attachment style? How do you think that might impact upon therapy?

continued overleaf

> Based on these reflections, do you think Sarah would benefit from counselling/psychotherapy? If so, what could be the advantages and disadvantages of:
>
> - a holding agreement?
> - a mini-agreement?
> - referral for ongoing therapy?
>
> If you thought that Sarah would need to be referred on, which agency would you refer her to?
>
> Sarah has not had many experiences of supportive relationships in her life, and that is likely to present a challenge to developing a relationship with a therapist. What do you think would be the characteristics of the approach that would suit her best?

COMMENT

The case study demonstrates some of the complex factors the assessor needs to consider in making a decision about an assessment. There is no 'right' course of action, and the questions posed in Activity 6.2 suggest some areas for consideration. You might think of other areas for exploration with your own clients.

THE ASSESSOR'S ROLE AND THE IMPACT ON ASSESSORS

Assessors within organisational settings have an important role. They offer the first clinical contact to clients; through this they represent the organisation and they may be the first contact a client has with the counselling world. The assessment session is a potential route to treatment and often represents the hope of change and healing.

All these aspects of the role mean that the assessment relationship is complex and involves a delicate balance between creating a safe and trusting environment, being a gatekeeper to the service and enabling a client to move on and attach to the therapist. In our collaborative enquiry at MCPS the assessors reflected on aspects of this process as well as the impact of conducting assessments on the assessor.

One of the important aspects of assessment is that the assessor is seen as a figure of authority but also as a trustworthy person, in a way that does not usually happen with a therapist at the beginning of the therapeutic relationship.

> *Assessor 2*: I think it's amazing how much people actually give, reveal about themselves in such a short period of time. How much trust they have.
>
> *Assessor 3*: Well, I hadn't thought about that so much until fairly recently when there seemed to be a succession of clients that made the very same comment: 'I've told you more in the last twenty minutes than I've told anybody' or 'I don't know you but I've told you things that I've never told anybody else' or 'I've only told one other person and that was ten years ago'.

This is a repeating pattern in organisational assessments. The confidential setting and the experience of being listened to, sometimes for the first time, highlight the intensity of the experience. The relative anonymity and brevity of the relationship seem to serve the same purpose, facilitating the extent of the potential disclosure for clients.

> *Supervisor*: Clients don't always do that with their therapists, as you well know. It takes time.
>
> *Assessor 2*: Oh right, so you are wondering why. Because there is not going to be a relationship, perhaps. There'll be no ramifications, no implications, no consequences, no judgement, whatever. It's just in that space.

To summarise, these examples highlight some of the differences between being an assessor and being a therapist.

- The intensity, the brevity and the formality of the assessment process have the potential to facilitate a high degree of disclosure, which does not usually happen in the first session with a client.
- The personality of the assessor and the relationship formed in the assessment highlight some of the central relationship themes for the client. Assessors use this relationship to help a client make the move from the assessment context to counselling.

In the previous chapters we have reflected on how the relationship with the assessor can be used as an assessment tool. The area of assessment that is often left unexplored is the emotional impact of this type of single session assessment on the assessors. In ongoing therapeutic relationships self-care of the therapist is clearly attended to and practitioners engage in ongoing clinical supervision and periods of personal therapy.

ASSESSMENT SKILLS

Assessors in organisations hear numerous accounts of human pain. They hear detailed experiences of abuse and human suffering. In order to assess the core issues with clients they engage emotionally in the assessment relationship, reflect on the themes within it and resonate with the emotions. The levels of distress they witness have a potential to create a range of emotional responses.

> *Assessor 1*: I just feel like I'm kind of in the assessment. It's like I'm completely sort of in their film or in their world and I'm sort of looking around and I can see when they were five or I can see when they were fifteen. Do you know what I mean? And there are all these, you know, it's like a big house, and then you are looking at all the, the levels of the house. Whereas when you're doing one-to-one therapy you might go to the second floor and have a little potter around. You are not going through all the levels at the same time and when I'm impacted I get quite immersed and I see so many pictures and that's the bit I find quite difficult 'cos I don't know whether it's because I've got a strong imagination or something but I see so many pictures that sometimes I just don't know what to do with that.

Another assessor reflects on the impact and the complexity of assessment:

> *Assessor 2*: What I'm seeing is so obvious in a way. Then I hear – it's like the pack of cards, you know. You sort of, it just becomes so obvious and you think, of course, you know this person's not been held all their life or – or even when initially I ask about their childhood they go 'Oh you know it's fine' and then suddenly the bits come out. And it's really hard not to feel impacted by that. And there are certain clients where I felt . . . [deep sigh] . . . a feeling. A real sort of feeling of the client. That I think is about me, in the moment. I think it's really, very demanding. Because there's so much that happens in that fifty minutes. There isn't yet a relationship. There's holding, there's writing, being responsible.

Stress levels involved in conducting a number of assessments cannot be ignored and have a potential impact of vicarious traumatisation on the assessors. Over the year of conducting this enquiry the assessors reported a number of emotional responses related to the assessments: dreams of traumatic narratives, a sense of hopelessness in the face of human suffering, feeling drained and vulnerable and losing confidence. Assessments sometimes brought up painful personal issues.

These areas of impact have been repeated in subsequent years, with different groups of trainee assessors. They also resonated with me during the period in which I conducted a large number of assessments.

This impact highlights the importance of self-care and stress management for the assessors. Clinical supervision can have an important role in this process. In my experience as a supervisor I found it useful to use the restorative functions of supervision (Proctor, 1997) and normalise experiences of being impacted and feeling vulnerable. In this way the supervision process can help assessors to gain more confidence in hearing different human experiences, particularly in the area of abuse and trauma.

> *Assessor 2*: And certainly there are certain types of clients' presentation that seem to hold more potential for me to be traumatised. Often they're the ones who can't move on that seem to affect me more. I feel more uncomfortable, uneasy or confused about the story. And then I think there is always going to be the odd client where the story is quite close to mine.
>
> *Assessor 1*: There have been some times when they've gone away and I've felt quite breathless and I've had asthmatic responses, but I haven't had that recently. You know, there is something about becoming a bit more immune.
>
> *Supervisor*: And maybe it's about finding that balance between empathy and distance.

Balancing the engagement with a client and individual separateness in the assessment process is also important in maintaining self-care. Assessors have found it useful to consciously embrace their own individuality, their lives and relationships, as a way of looking after themselves.

ACTIVITY 6.3
- Think about clinical issues that might make a particular impact on you. Are there areas of conflict, abuse and trauma you might have experienced?
- Think of a period when you experienced a high degree of stress in your life. What might be the behaviours, thoughts and feelings you can identify as signals of stress?
- Identify areas of support for yourself, both professionally and personally.

CHAPTER SUMMARY

- In this chapter we have suggested that conducting assessments requires some specific skills that can facilitate the session and enable the assessor to gain relevant information while maintaining clients' safety.
- Balancing containment with listening facilitates the establishment of a working relationship while maintaining the boundaries, focusing on client's safety and avoiding retraumatisation.
- Probing enables the assessor to follow up the themes that emerge during the assessment and develop an understanding of the client's presenting issues.
- Two types of questionnaires could be used in the assessment: standardised questionnaires, which can help to develop diagnosis, assess risk and evaluate therapy; and personal details questionnaires, which can help to speed up the information-gathering required for the assessment. There is evidence that the use of questionnaires can have benefits as well as disadvantages (Mace, 1995b). Using questionnaires collaboratively with clients and paying attention to confidentiality and the fear of judgement could help to deal with the potential disadvantages and enhance the assessment process.
- Reflexive questions and case studies give you an opportunity to explore how you might think about and use these skills in your own assessment practice.
- The chapter also highlights the importance of self-care for assessors and suggests that the assessment process contains particular stressors for the assessors.

SUGGESTED FURTHER READING

Elton Wilson, J (1996) *Time-conscious psychological therapy.* London: Routledge.

This offers a useful format to developing contract with clients.

Mace, C (1995) When are questionnaires helpful? in Mace, C (ed) *The art and science of assessment in psychotherapy.* London: Routledge.

This reflects on the use of questionnaires in assessment.

Rothschild, B (2000) *The body remembers: the psychophysiology of trauma and trauma treatment.* New York: WW Norton.

This gives an insight into the impact of trauma and can be used to identify symptoms of trauma.

APPENDIX 1

Initial assessment form used by the Metanoia Counselling and Psychotherapy Service

A Contact details

| Client ref no: | First contact: |

| Date of assessment: |

| Client name: |

| Address:
Postcode:
Tel no:
Age: |

| GP details: |

| Assessor: |

| Referred to: |

Date of first appointment:

Day: Monday   Tuesday   Wednesday   Thursday   Friday

Time: am /pm

Notes: Make a note if the client was not taken into the service, whether they were referred on elsewhere and where they were referred to.

B Personal details

Ref no.

PRESENTING ISSUES AND CURRENT CIRCUMSTANCES

Why therapy? Why now?

General functioning information: work, current relationships, support network.

DSM-IV diagnostic categories for consideration: Axis I and Axis V

Ability for a coherent narrative and reflection

FAMILY BACKGROUND AND PERSONAL HISTORY

Factual information – who was around, order of birth in the family, broadly based personal history

DSM-IV diagnostic categories for consideration:
    Axis I – trauma, mental health issues
    Axis II – personality disorders and traits

Ability for a coherent narrative and reflection

QUESTIONNAIRES

List the mean scores

Pay attention to clinical/non-clinical categories

Always explore risk if indicated

COUNSELLING/PSYCHOTHERAPY HISTORY

Where?

How long for?

Was it helpful?

Give information about counselling

Answer queries

AIMS STATED

Beginning to formulate the treatment contract

STATE OF HEALTH

Alcohol intake: *how much? / how often?/ recent changes?*

Smoking: *how much? / how often? / recent changes?*

Use of drugs: *how much? / how often? / recent changes?*

Other:

Pay attention to substance abuse and Axis III categories

References

Alberts, G (1998) Feelings for the patient, in Rabinowitz, I (ed) *Inside therapy: illuminating writings about therapists, patients and psychotherapy*. New York: St Martin's Griffin, pp99–115.

Alvesson, M and Skoldeberg, K (2000) *Reflexive methodology*. London: Sage.

American Psychiatric Association (2000) *DSM-IV-TR*. New York: APA.

Argyris, C, and Schön, D (1978) *Organizational learning: a theory of action perspective*. Reading, MA: Addison Wesley.

Aveline, M (1997) Assessing for optimal therapeutic intervention, in Palmer, S and McMahon, G (eds) *Client assessment*. London: Sage, pp93–114.

BACP (2010) *Ethical framework for good practice in counselling and psychotherapy*. Lutterworth: British Association for Counselling & Psychotherapy.

Bager-Charleson S (2010a) *Reflective practice in counselling and psychotherapy*. Exeter: Learning Matters.

Bager-Charleson S (2010b) (ed) *Why therapists choose to become therapists*. London: Karnac.

Barkham, M, Margison, F, Leach, C, Lucock, MJ, Mellor-Clark, J and Evans, C (2001) Service profiling and outcomes benchmarking using the CORE-OM: toward practice-based evidence in the psychological therapies. *Journal of Consulting and Clinical Psychology*, 69: 184–96.

Barkham, M, Hardy, G and Mellor-Clark, J (2010) *Developing and delivering practice-based evidence*. Chichester: Wiley-Blackwell.

Bateman, A and Holmes, J (2002) *Introduction to psychoanalysis: contemporary theory and practice*. Hove: Brunner-Routledge.

Beck, A (2006) *Depression: causes and treatment*. Philadelphia, PA: University of Pennsylvania Press.

Berne, E (1966) *Principles of group treatment*. New York: Oxford University Press.

Berne, E (1972) *What do you say after you say hello?* New York: Grove Press.

Beutler, LE (1989) Differential treatment selection: the role of diagnosis in psychotherapy. *Psychotherapy*, 26(3): 271–81.

Beutler, LE, Machado PP and Neufeldt, S (1994) Therapist variables, in Bergin, NA and Garfield, SL (eds) *Handbook of psychotherapy and behaviour change* (4th edition). Chichester: John Wiley, pp229–70.

Beutler, LE, Malik, M, Alimohamed, S, Harwood, TM, Talebi, H, Noble, S et al. (2004) Therapist variables, in Lambert, MJ (ed) *Handbook of psychotherapy and behaviour change* (5th edition). Chichester: John Wiley and Sons.

Bion, W (1962) *Learning from experience*. London: Karnac.

Blatt, SJ, Sanislow, CA, Zuroff, DC and Pilkonis, PA (1996) Impact of perfectionism and the need for approval on the brief treatment for depression. *Journal of Consulting and Clinical Psychology*, 66(2): 423–28.

Bolton, G (2005) *Reflective practice – writing and professional development*. London: Sage.

Bowlby, J (1982) *Attachment and loss Vol 1: Attachment*. London: Hogarth Press and the Institute of Psychoanalysis.

Cardinal, J, Hayward, J and Jones, G (2004) *Epistemology – the theory of knowledge*. London: John Murray.

Casement, P (2008) *Learning from life: becoming a psychoanalyst*. London and New York: Routledge.

Cashdan, S (1988) *Object relation therapy: using the relationship*. Ontario: Penguin.

Claringbull, N (2011) *Mental health in counselling and psychotherapy*. Exeter: Learning Matters.

Clarksson, P (1995) *The therapeutic relationship*. London: Whurr Publishers.

Cooper, M (2008) *Essential research findings in counselling and psychotherapy: the facts are friendly*. London: Sage.

Cooper, H and Alfillé, H (eds) (1998) *Assessment in psychotherapy*. London: Karnac.

Cozolino, L (2002) *The neuroscience of psychotherapy: building and rebuilding the human brain*. New York: Norton Press.

CSIP (Care Services Improvement Partnership) (2008) *Improving access to psychological therapies* (IAPT) commissioning toolkit, April. NB: The CSIP was closed in 2008.

Cummings, NA and VandenBos, GR (1979) The general practice of psychology. *Professional Psychology*, 10: 430–40.

Curwen, B (1997) Medical and psychiatric assessment, in Palmer, S and McMahon, G (eds) *Client assessment*. London: Sage.

Daines, B, Gask, L and Howe, A (2007) *Medical and psychiatric issues for counsellors*. London: Sage.

Dale, H (2008) *Making the contract for counselling and psychotherapy*. Lutterworth: BACP.

Da Rocha Barros, EM (2002) First interview and one session with 'Ana'. *International Journal of Psycho-Analysis*, 83: 569–74.

Davies, TO, Nutley, S and Smith, PC (2000) What works? *Evidence-based policy and practice in public services*. London: Policy Press.

Denford, J (1995) How I assess for inpatient psychotherapy, in Mace, C (ed) *The art and science of assessment in psychotherapy*. London: Routledge, pp42–60.

Denman, C (1995) What is the point of a formulation? in Mace, C (ed) *The art and science of assessment in psychotherapy*. London: Routledge, pp167–81.

Despenser, S (2007) Risk assessment: the personal safety of the counsellor. *BACP: Therapy Today*, March: 12–13.

REFERENCES

DuBrin, JR and Zastowny, TR (1988) Predicting early attrition from psychotherapy: an analysis of a large private practice cohort. *Psychotherapy*, 25(3): 394–408.

Eagle, MN (2006) Attachment, psychotherapy, and assessment: a commentary. *Journal of Consulting and Clinical Psychology*, 74(6): 1086–97.

Egan, G (1985) *The skilled helper*. Belmont, CA: Wadsworth Publishing Co.

Elfant, AB (1985) Psychotherapy and assessment in hospital settings: ideological and professional conflicts. *Professional Psychology: Research and Practice*, 16: 55–63.

Elton Wilson, J (1996) *Time-conscious psychological therapy*. London: Routledge.

Etherington, K (2004) *Becoming a reflexive researcher: using our selves in research*. London and Philadelphia, PA: Jessica Kingsley.

Finlay, L and Gough, B (2003) *Reflexivity: a practical guide for researchers in health and social science*. London: Blackwell.

Friedman, M (1999) *The worlds of existentialism*. New York: Humanity Books.

Gabriel, L and Casemore, R (2010) *Guidance for ethical decision making: a suggested model for practitioners*. P4 Information sheet. Lutterworth: BACP.

Gardner, F (2008) Using critical reflection in research and valuation, in White, S, Fook, J and Gardner, F (eds) *Critical reflection in health and social care*. Maidenhead: Open University Press.

Green, J (2010) *Creating the therapeutic relationship in counselling and pyschotherapy*. Exeter: Learning Matters.

Green, V (ed) (2003) *Emotional development in psychoanalysis, attachment theory and neuroscience: creating connections*. London and New York: Routledge.

Greenberg, M, Sukhwinder, S, Szmukler, G and Tantam, D (2003) *Narratives in psychiatry*. London: Jessica Kingsley.

Guggenbühl-Craig, A (2009) *Power in the helping professions*. New York: Spring Publications.

Hawkins, P and Shohet, R (2006) *Supervision in the helping professions*. Maidenhead: Open University Press.

Hemmings, A and Field, R (2007) *Counselling and psychotherapy in contemporary private practice*. London and New York: Routledge.

Heron, J and Reason, P (2001) The practice of co-operative inquiry: research with rather than on people, in Reason, P and Bradbury, H (eds) *Handbook of action research: participative inquiry and practice*. London: Sage Publications, pp179–88.

Hinshelwood, RD (1995) Psychodynamic formulation in assessment for psychoanalytic psychotherapy, in Mace, C (ed) *The art and science of assessment in Psychotherapy*. London and New York: Routledge, pp155–66.

Hoffman, S and Weinberger, J (2007) *The art and science of psychotherapy*. London and New York: Routledge.

Holmes, J. (1995) How I assess for psychoanalytical psychotherapy, in Mace, C (ed) *The art and science of assessment in psychotherapy*. London and New York: Routledge, pp27–41.

Holmes, J and Bateman, A (eds) (2002) *Integration in psychotherapy: models and methods*. New York: Oxford University Press.

Holmes, J and Lindley, R (1998) *The value of psychotherapy*. London: Karnac.

Jenkins, P (2007) *Counselling, psychotherapy and the law* (2nd edition). London: Sage.

Johnstone, L and Dallos, R (eds) (2006) *Formulation in psychotherapy and psychology: making sense of people's problems*. London and New York: Routledge.

Kantrowitz, JL, Katz, AL and Paolitto, F (1990) Followup of psychoanalysis five to ten years after termination: I. Stability of change. *Journal of American Psychoanalytic Association*, 38: 471–96.

Kottler, JA (1993) *On being a therapist*. San Francisco, CA: Jossey-Bass Publishers.

Kvale, S (ed) (1999) *Psychology and postmodernism*. London: Sage.

Lambert, MJ and Ogles, BM (2004) The efficacy and effectiveness of psychotherapy, in Lambert, MJ (ed) *Bergin and Garfield's handbook of psychotherapy and behaviour change* (5th edition). Chicago, IL: Wiley and Sons.

Loewenthal, D and Snell, R (2003) *Postmodernism for psychotherapists: a critical reader*. Hover and New York: Brunner-Routledge.

Luborsky, L and Singer, B (1975) Comparative studies of psychotherapies: is it true that 'everyone has won and all must have prizes'? *Archives of General Psychiatry*, 32: 995–1008.

Luborsky, L, McLellan, AT, Woody, GE, O'Brien, CP and Auerbach, A (1985) Therapist success and its determinants. *Archives of General Psychiatry*, 42(6): 602–11.

Mace, C (ed) (1995a) *The art and science of assessment in psychotherapy*. London: Routledge.

Mace, C (1995b) When are questionnaires helpful? in Mace, C (ed) *The art and science of assessment in psychotherapy*. London: Routledge, pp203–225.

Malan, DH (1979) *Individual psychotherapy and the science of psychodynamics*. London: Butterworths.

Malovic-Yeeles, M (1998) Contradictions for psychodynamic psychotherapy, in Cooper, J and Alfillé, H (eds) *Assessment in psychotherapy*. London: Karnac, pp125–34.

Marquis, A (2008) *The integral intake: a guide to comprehensive idiographic assessment in integral psychotherapy*. New York: Routledge, Taylor and Francis.

Mash, EJ and Hunsley, J (1993) Assessment considerations in the assessment of failing psychotherapy: bringing the negatives out of the darkroom. *Psychological Assessment*, 5(3): 292–301.

McBride, C, Atkinson, L, Quilty, LC and Bagby, RM (2006) Attachment as moderator of treatment outcome in major depression: a randomized control trial of interpersonal psychotherapy versus cognitive–behavioral therapy. *Journal of Consulting and Clinical Psychology*, 74: 1041–54.

McLeod, J (1997) *Narrative and psychotherapy*: London: Sage.

REFERENCES

McMahon, G (2009) Client history taking and associated administration, in Palmer, G and McMahon, G (eds), *Client assessment*. London: Sage, pp29–46.

Meyer, B and Pilkonis, PA (2002) Attachment style, in Norcross, JC (ed) *Psychotherapy relationships that work: therapist contributions and responsiveness to patients*. New York: Oxford University Press, pp367–82.

Miller, A (1997) *The drama of the gifted child: the search for the true self*. Translated from German by R Ward. New York: HarperCollins.

Milner, J and O'Byrne, P (2004) *Assessment in counselling: theory, process and decision making*. Basingstoke: Palgrave Macmillan.

Mitchels, B and Bond, T (2010) *Essential law for counsellors and psychotherapists*. Los Angeles, CA and London: Sage.

Mohr, JJ, Gelso, CJ and Hill, CE (2005) Client and counsellor trainee: attachment as predictors of session evaluation and countertransference behaviour in first counselling sessions. *Journal of Counselling Psychology*, 5(3): 298–309.

NICE (2007) *Management of depression in primary and secondary care* (April). Available online at www.nice.org.uk/CG23 (replaced by CG 90).

Norcross, JC (ed) (2002) *Psychotherapy relationships that work: therapist contributions and responsiveness to patients*. New York: Oxford University Press.

O'Hanlon, B and Bertolino, B (1998) *Even from a broken web: Brief, respectful solution-oriented therapy for sexual abuse and trauma*. New York: Wiley.

Orlinsky, D, Grawe, K and Parks, B (1994) Process and outcome in psychotherapy-noch einmal, in Bergin, AE and Garfield, SL (eds) *Handbook of psychotherapy and behaviour change*. Chicago, IL: John Wiley and Sons, pp270–6.

Page, S (1999) *The shadow and the counsellor*. London and New York: Routledge.

Parker, I (1994) Qualitative research, in Banister, B et al. *Qualitative methods in psychology: a research guide*. Buckingham: Open University Press.

Parker, I (2004) *Qualitative psychology: introducing radical research*. New York: Open University Press.

Paul, GL (1967) Strategy of outcome research in psychotherapy. *Journal of Consulting Psychology*, 31: 109–18.

Prochaska, JO (1984) *Systems of psychotherapy: a transtheoretical analysis*, Homewood, IL: Dorsey Press.

Prochaska, JO and DiClemente, CC (1992) The transtheoretical approach, in Norcross, JC and Goldfried, MR (eds) *Handbook of psychotherapy integration*. New York: Basic Books, pp300–34.

Proctor, B (1986) Supervision: a co-operative exercise in accountability, in Marken, M and Payne, M (eds) *Enabling and ensuring: supervision in practice*. Leicester: National Youth Bureau.

Proctor, B (1997) *Contracts in supervision*, in Sills, C (ed) *Contracts in counselling*. London: Sage, pp190–206.

Rabinowitz, I (ed) (1998) *Inside therapy: illuminating writings about therapists, patients and psychotherapy*. New York: St Martin's Griffin.

Ricoeur, P (1998) *Hermeneutics and the human sciences*. Thomson (transl. and ed) Cambridge: Cambridge University Press.

Roffey-Barentsen, J and Malthouse, R (2009) *Reflective practice in the lifelong learning sector*. Exeter: Learning Matters.

Rogers, C (1961) *A therapist's view of psychotherapy*. London: Constable and Co.

Rosen, H and Kuehlwein, K (eds) (1996) *Constructing realities – meaning making perspectives for psychotherapists*. San Francisco, CA: Jossey Bass.

Rosenfield, M (1997) *Counselling by telephone*. London: Sage.

Roth, A and Fonagy, P (2005) *What works for whom? A critical review of psychotherapy research*. New York: Guilford Press.

Rothschild, B (2000) *The body remembers: the psychophysiology of trauma and trauma treatment*. New York: WW Norton.

Ruddell, P (2009) *General assessment issues*, in Palmer, S and McMahon, G (eds) *Client assessment*. London: Sage, pp6–28.

Ruddell, P and Curwen, B (1997) What type of help? in Palmer, S and McMahon, G (eds) *Client assessment*. London and New York: Sage, pp73–92.

Ryle, A and Kerr, IB (2002) *Introducing cognitive analytic therapy: principles and practice*. New York: Wiley.

Safran, JD and Muran, JC (2003) *Negotiating the therapeutic alliance*. New York: Guilford Press.

Sarup, M (1993) *An introductory guide to post-structuralism and postmodernism*. Harlow: Pearson Education.

Schön, DA (1983) *The reflective practitioner: how professionals think in action*. New York: Basic Books.

Schön, D and Rein, M (1994) *Frame reflection: towards the resolution of intractable policy controversies*. New York: Basic Books.

Sedgwick, D (1994) *The wounded healer: countertransference from a Jungian perspective*. London and New York: Routledge.

Sills, C (1997) Contracts and contract making, in Sills, C (ed) *Contracts in counselling*. London: Sage, pp11–33.

Spinelli, E (1997) *Tales of un-knowing: therapeutic encounters from an existential perspective*. New York: New York University Press.

Strean, H (1998) Sometimes I feel like a dirty old man; the woman who tried to seduce me, in Rabinowitz, I (ed) *Inside therapy: illuminating writings about therapists, patients and psychotherapy*. New York: St Martin's Griffin, pp116–31.

Strupp, H and Binder, J (1984) *Psychotherapy in a new key: a guide to time-limited dynamic psychotherapy*. New York: Basic Books.

Sussman, MB (1992) *A curious calling – unconscious motivations for practising psychotherapy*. New York and London: Jason Aronson.

Symington, N (1986) *The analytic experience: lectures from the Tavistock*. London: Free Association Books.

Tantum, D (1995) Why assess? in Mace, C (ed) *The art and science of assessment in psychotherapy*. London: Routledge, pp8–26.

Taylor, B (2006) *Reflective practice: a guide for nurses and midwives*. Maidenhead: Open University Press.

Tindall, C (1994) Personal construct approaches, in Banister, B, Burman, F, Parker, I, Taylor, M and Tindall, C (eds) *Qualitative methods in psychology: a research guide*. Buckingham: Open University Press, pp72–91.

Tseng, W-S and Streltzer, J (eds) (1997) *Culture and psychotherapy: a guide to clinical assessment*. New York: Brunner/Mazel.

Valbak, K (2004) Suitability for psychoanalytic psychotherapy: a review. *Acta Psychiatrica Scandinavica*, 109(3): 164–78.

Van Deurzen, E (2009) *Existential therapy*. Available online at www.existentialpsychotherapy.net/.

Van Rijn, B (2010) Evaluating our practice, in Bager-Charleson (ed) *Reflective practice in counselling and psychotherapy*. Exeter: Learning Matters, pp111–20

Wallin, DJ (2007) *Attachment in psychotherapy*. London, New York: Guilford Press.

Wampold, B (2001) *The great psychotherapy debate*. Mahwah, NJ: Lawrence Erlbaum Associates.

White, J (2006) *Generation: preoccupations and conflicts in contemporary psychoanalysis*. Hove: Routledge.

White, S, Fook, J and Gardner, F (eds) (2008) *Critical reflection in health and social care*. Maidenhead: Open University.

Winnicott, DW (1965) *The maturational process and the facilitating environment*. London: Karnac.

Withers, M (2007) Assessment, in Hemmings, A and Field, R (eds) *Counselling and psychotherapy in contemporary private practice*. Hove: Routledge.

Wolberg, L (1977) *The technique of psychotherapy*, New York: Grune & Stratton.

Wosket, V (1999) *The therapeutic use of self-counselling practice, research and supervision*. London and New York: Routledge.

Yalom, I. (1980) *Existential psychotherapy*. New York: Basic Books.

Index

A
ABC model 38–40
abortion 50–1, 52–3
acceptance 92
action stage, change 97
advertising 31
Ainsworth, Mary 99
'alchemic' process 3
Alfillé, Helen 40, 41
alpha function 71
American Psychiatric Association (APA) 45
anonymity, telephone assessment 85
Argyris, Chris 51, 72
'assessment' concept 45
   difference from 'diagnosis' 102–3
assessments, preliminary 92–3
attachment 99–100, 104, 111, 117
attribution, therapeutic outcome 74
autonomy 15, 21, 22, 26
Aveline, Mark 22, 33, 36–7, 41, 58
awareness 12, 68, 79

B
BACP ethical framework 20–1
Barkham, Michael 49
Bateman, Anthony 44–5, 65, 70, 73
Beck Depression Inventory (BDI) 74, 114–15
behavioural approaches 73–4
beliefs *see* values and beliefs
beneficence 21, 22, 26, 48
Berne, Eric 4, 79
Bertolino, Bob 16
beta-elements, memories as 71
biases/blind spots 2, 3, 4, 16, 17–18, 19, 23, 53, 70
Binder, Jeffrey 40–1
Bion, Wilfred 64–5, 71–2
Bond, Tim 31–2
boundaries *see* containment
Bowlby, John 99
brief therapy 84, 84–5
British Association for Counselling and Psychotherapy (BACP) ethical framework 20–1
Buber, Martin 66

C
Cardinal, Daniel 48
Casement, Patrick 53
Cashdan, Sheldon 70
CAT *see* cognitive analytical therapy
'cause' 72, 93

CBT *see* cognitive behavioural therapy
change 72
   ABC model 38–40
   cost of 40–1
   levels of 97
   and loss 37–8
   stages of 96–8
choice 2, 22, 86
   and expectations 31
   and financial dynamics 11
   treatment options 118
Clarksson, Petruska 41, 66
classification, mental health disorders 45–6
client factors, outcomes 116–17
client relationships 103
clinical diagnosis 14, 45–6, 102–6
cognitions, maladaptive 97
cognitive analytical therapy (CAT) 72
cognitive behavioural therapy (CBT) 68, 74
common factor theory 73–4, 117
commonalities, finding 45
confidentiality 32–3, 61, 81, 114
conflicts 37, 97
conscious/unconscious expectations 28
consent 32
constructivism 3
containment 110, 111–12
contemplation stage, change 96
contracts 31–33, 79
   contractual themes 32–3
Cooper, Judy 40, 41
'core conditions', person-centred therapy 67
CORE-OM (Clinical Outcomes in Routine Evaluation – Outcome Measure) 35, 46–8, 88, 114–15
'core' symptoms 49
countertransference 15–16, 70, 77–9
   and attachment 100
   and formulation 104–5
   see also transference
couple therapy 37–8, 38–40, 56–7
critical friends 4, 12, 52
cultural biases *see* biases/blind spots
curiosity, engaging with 40–1
Curwen, Berni 40, 41, 107

D
Daines, Brian 34, 60–1
Dale, Heather 32–3
Dallos, Rudi 44, 75
Davies, Huw 49

INDEX

defences, against change 37–40
Denford, John 93–4, 99, 112
Denman, Chess 103
depression, Beck Depression Inventory 74, 114–15
Despenser, Sally 23–4, 59–60
detachment 27, 108
'diagnosis' concept 6, 44, 45
   difference from 'assessment' 102–3
   see also clinical diagnosis
Diagnostic and statistical manual of mental disorders (DSM-IV) 45–6
   see also clinical diagnosis
DiClemente, Carlo 96–7
'digestion' 71
Dilthey, Wilhelm 54
disclosure, containment 111–12
discrimination 23
'double-loop' assessment/learning 5, 12–13, 18–19, 36, 52, 58, 70, 79–81
DSM-IV 45–6

E
EBT *see* evidence-based treatment
educational institutions 84
ego strength 37, 40
Elton Wilson, Jenifer 118
emotional stability 37
emotions 15–16, 121–2
   as personal possessions 71
   and telephone assessment 87
empathy 92
empirically supported treatment (EST) 49
epistemology 55
Erklärung/Verstehen 54, 55, 75
espoused theory 51–2, 72–3
ethics 15, 20–3, 25–6, 48, 74–5, 81
   conflict between guidelines 61–2
   see also risk assessment
evaluating 93
'evidence'
   and epistemology 55
   meaning of 49
evidence-based treatment (EBT) 49
existential therapy 65–7
expectations 73
   conscious/unconscious 28
   from prior relationships 29–30
   unrealistic 31–2
experiential/humanistic approaches 73–4
exposure 74

F
face-to-face assessments 89
fantasies 28, 87
   'ultimate parent' 28, 31
feedback 19–20
feelings *see* emotions
fidelity 21, 25
Field, Rosalind 16
financial dynamics 11
fluid contracts 33

formative needs 19
'formulation' 14–15, 44–5
   using countertransference 104–5
   see also hypotheses
framing 2, 17, 54, 67, 71
Freud, Sigmund 15, 28, 29

G
Gardner, Fiona 12
Green, Judith 10, 73
Green, Viviane 72
Guggenbühl-Craig, Adolf 12
guidelines
   BACP ethical framework 20–1
   conflict between 61–2

H
health issues 94
'helping' 69–71
Hemmings, Adrian 16
higher education services 84
Hinshelwood, Robert 48, 65, 67, 71, 103
histories, personal/therapeutic 94
   see also narratives
history taking 92, 100–1
Hoffman, Stefan 73–4
Holmes, Jeremy 29, 34, 44–5, 65, 70, 73, 78, 87
honesty 12
'hooks' 69–70
humanistic/experiential approaches 73–4
Hume, David 72
hypotheses 44–5, 48
   as 'markers' 6, 67, 71

I
I–Thou relationship 66
IAPT (Improving Access to Psychological Therapies) services, stepped care model 82, 83
identification, projective 70
'ideographic' assessment 54
information 93
   'sieving' for 6, 46–7, 49–51, 75
informed decisions 22
integration-in-practice 73
interviews
   first meetings 8–10, 23–4, 29–30, 35, 36, 44–5, 46–7
   primary goals 92–3
   structuring 93–6
involvement 116

J
Jenkins, Peter 11, 20–1, 23, 25, 32, 61
Johnstone, Lucy 44, 75
justice 21, 23, 26

K
Kächele, Horst 41
Kerr, Ian 72

'knowing' 53, 71
　'not knowing', existentialism 66
'knowledge', meaning of 48
Kvale, Steinar 13–14

L
Lacan, Jacques 17
law 20–1
liability 11
life scripts 4
Lindley, Richard 29, 78, 87
listening skills 87
　and containment 110, 111–12
locus of evaluation 51–2
Loewenthal, Del 14
loss, and change 37–8

M
Mace, Chris 34, 114
maintenance stage, change 97
maladaptive cognitions 97
Malan, David 92
Malovic-Yeeles, Mira 24
'markers' 6, 67, 71, 75
marketing 31
Marquis, Andre 54
mastery 74
maximum pain, point of 47, 65, 103
McBride, Carolina 104
McLeod, John 99
McMahon, Gladeana 92
meanings, co-creating 65–71
medication/health issues 94
memories, as beta-elements 71
mental health disorders, classification 45–6
metacognition 68
Metanoia Counselling and Psychotherapy Service (MCPS) 5, 91, 94, 125–7
Milner, Judith 17, 18, 34
'minimum intervention' principle 22
Mitchels, Barbara 31–2
motivation 96–8, 116
　therapists 24, 25
Muran, J Christopher 13, 14

N
narratives 115
　in assessment sessions 101–2
　role of 98–101
neuroscience 72
'nomothetic' assessment 54
non-maleficence 21, 22–3, 26, 48
non-statutory organisations 84–5
normative needs 19

O
O'Byrne, Patrick 17, 18, 34
O'Hanlon, Bill 16
'one-person' psychologies 15

organisations, assessment in 6–7, 81–5
　assessor's role 120–3
　face-to-face assessments 89
　telephone assessments 85–9
'organismic self' concept 67
outcomes 49, 73
　attribution 74
　client factors 116–17
　promises/contracts 31–3, 79
　referrals 58, 60–1, 82, 84, 115–16
　therapeutic approach 117
　therapist factors 117
　treatment options 118–20

P
pain, maximum point of 47, 65, 103
perfectionism 116
person-centred therapy 50–52, 53–4, 67
person-to-person relationship 66
personal crises, therapists 24
personal histories 94
　see also narratives
personal skills 87
personal therapy 25–8
placebo effect 73
'plumbing' metaphor 41
political agents, assessors as 17
'post-tribal' trend 73
postmodernism 13–14
power, abuse of 18
pre-assessment questionnaires 33–4
precontemplation stage, change 96, 98
preliminary assessments 92–3
preparation stage, change 97
presenting issues 94
private practice 5–6
　financial dynamics 11
　liability 11
　need for assessment 10
　risk assessment 40–1, 56–9
　see also ethics
probing skills 110, 112–14
process contracts 33
Prochaska, James 96–7
projective identification 70
psychoanalysis 28
psychodynamic therapy 3, 68, 70, 73–4
psychological functioning 116
psychological mindedness 116–17

Q
questionnaires 33–4, 49, 114–15
　CORE-OM 35, 46–8, 88, 114–15
　and narratives 100–1
　triage assessment 82

R
rapport 92
'readiness' for therapy 35–7
　cost of change 40–1
　resistance to change 37–40
referrals 58, 60–1, 82, 84, 115–16

reflective practice 12–13, 17, 18, 54, 70, 79, 104–5
   supervision 19–20, 52–3
reflexive awareness 12
reflexivity 5, 79–80
relational transactional analysis 4
relationships
   clients' 103
   and expectations 29–30
   therapeutic 73, 89
'rescuing trap' 24, 25, 69–71
restorative needs 19–20
Ricoeur, Paul 54
risk assessment 40–1, 56–9
   conflict between guidelines 61–2
   suicide 107–8
   violence 59–60, 113–14
risk-taking, therapists 23–4
Rogers, Carl 53–4
Rosenfield, Maxine 86–7
Roy-Chowdhury, S 44
Ruddell, Peter 40, 41, 45
Ryle, Anthony 72

S
safety, therapists 23–4
   see also risk assessment
Safran, Jeremy D 13, 14
Schön, Donald 13, 51, 54, 67, 72, 79
school counselling 84
Sedgwick, David 70
self-actualisation 67
self-awareness 12, 68, 79
self-care 121–3
   see also risk assessment
self-respect 21, 23, 74–5
'shadows' 2, 69–70
'sieving' for information 6, 46–7, 49–51, 75
signs *see* symptoms and signs
'single-loop' learning 52–3
situational problems 97
Snell, Robert 14
social constructionism 3
social role(s), assessors 17–19
social skills 87
statutory sector 82–4, 102
stepped care model 82–3
Strean, Herbert 26
Streltzer, Jon 17
strengths/weaknesses, assessing 93
stress management 122–3
Strupp, Hans 40–1
substance abuse 97–8, 113
suicide 107–8
supervision 19–20, 52–3
symptoms and signs 45, 97
   'core' symptoms 49

T
TA *see* transactional analysis
Taylor, Beverly 12
telephone assessment 85–9
'theoretical' countertransference 16
'theory-in-use' 51–2
therapeutic approach, outcomes 117
therapeutic histories 94
therapeutic outcome, attribution of 74
therapeutic relationships 73, 89
therapist factors, outcomes 117
Thomä, Helmut 41
time boundaries 111
timekeeping, telephone assessment 87
time-limited therapy 84, 84–5
transactional analysis (TA) 4, 79
transference 28–30, 77–9, 87
   see also countertransference
transtheoretical approach 96–8
treatment options 118–20
triage assessment 82
trustworthiness 21
truth 3, 74
Tschudi, Finn, ABC model 38–40
Tseng, Wen-Shing 17
'two-person' psychologies 5, 13–15

U
'ultimate parent' fantasy 28, 31
unconscious expectations 28
'unconscious', shift in meaning 65
understanding with/about the client 54
university counselling services 84

V
values and beliefs 3, 14, 17, 40, 72, 92
   couple therapy 38
   and 'theory-in-use' 51–2
   see also 'double-loop' assessment
van Deurzen, Emmy 66
Verstehen/Erklärung 54, 55, 75
violence, assessing risk of 59–60, 113–14
voluntary organisations 84–5

W
Weinberger, Joel 73–4
Withers, Melanie 10–11, 13, 31
Wolberg, Lewis 92–3
Wosket, Val 73
'wounded healers' 25
'woundedness' 2

Y
Yalom, Irvin 65–6, 66–7